BLACK GIRL MAGIC BEYOND THE HASHTAG

THE FEMINIST WIRE BOOKS
Connecting Feminisms, Race, and Social Justice

BLACK GIRL
MAGIC
BEYOND THE
HASHTAG

Twenty-First-Century
Acts of Self-Definition

EDITED BY
JULIA S. JORDAN-ZACHERY
AND DUCHESS HARRIS

Foreword by Janell Hobson
Afterword by Tammy Owens

**THE UNIVERSITY OF
ARIZONA PRESS**
TUCSON

The University of Arizona Press
www.uapress.arizona.edu

© 2019 by The Arizona Board of Regents
All rights reserved. Published 2019

ISBN-13: 978-0-8165-3953-6 (paper)

Cover design by Leigh McDonald
Cover art: *Archetype of a 5 Star* by Jamea Richmond-Edwards. Rubell Family Collection,
courtesy of Kravets Wehby Gallery

Library of Congress Cataloging-in-Publication Data are available at the Library of Congress.

Printed in the United States of America
♾ This paper meets the requirements of ANSI/NISO Z39.48-1992 (Permanence of Paper).

To the Black women who worked tirelessly for me to experience "magic," thank you. To my daughter, Makeen, for pushing me to think critically, thanks.
—**JULIA JORDAN-ZACHERY**

For my favorite Black girl: Avi Noelle Thomas
—**DUCHESS HARRIS**

CONTENTS

FOREWORD

Janell Hobson

One would think the hashtag #BlackGirlMagic belongs to a community of Black women and girls. That is until both *Essence* magazine and Beverly Bond's Black Girls Rock! organization entered a trademark dispute for copyright ownership over the slogan in 2017. Somehow, CaShawn Thompson—credited with the slogan "Black Girls are Magic," which became a T-shirt logo that she designed—disappeared from the conversation, even though the viral hashtag #BlackGirlMagic arrived on the scene of Black Twitter soon after Thompson's logo and within the year of the creation of #BlackLivesMatter in 2013, which was first coined by three Black women, Alicia Garza, Patrisse Cullors, and Opal Tometi.

We may well debate just who "owns" the #BlackGirlMagic expression—as a shorthand description for any Black woman stylishly posing for Instagram selfies or fabulously dominating her profession if she happens to be a public figure in entertainment, sports, politics, activism, or the academy—but there is no doubt that it has entered the larger public domain empowering Black women and girls. Hashtag or trademark, personal or collective expression, #BlackGirlMagic is the articulation of the resolve and persistence of Black women and girls to triumph in the face of intersectional oppressions. The inter-twined effects of racism and sexism—defined by various Black feminists as "double jeopardy" (Frances Beale), "interlocking oppressions" (Combahee River), "matrix of domination" (Patricia Hill Collins), and "intersectionality" (Kimberlé Crenshaw)—oftentimes seem so insurmountable that any achievement on the part of Black women and girls cannot help but seem "magical." However, when we talk about BlackGirlMagic, we are merely defining the collective resistance of Black women and girls who dare to see themselves as beautiful and desirable in a culture that undermines their sex appeal, who dare to recognize their own brilliance in a society that constantly refutes their intellectual abilities, and who dare to revere their own communities, knowledge systems, and cultural practices in a nation that is determined to only view these entities through the lens of dysfunction.

The resistance of Black women and girls is a *magical* intervention into white supremacist and imperialist patriarchal narratives that extend earlier Black liberation projects challenging *rational* ideologies. As Trinh T. Minh-ha would argue, "black magic women" confound dominant narratives by preserving the power of oppositional speech acts (1989, 129). An ancient property wielded by ancient women, this "magic" takes on new life in the neoliberal spaces of digital culture that perpetually threaten to steal from, appropriate, and disavow the economic labor and cultural value of Black women and girls. The online life of #BlackGirlMagic insists on the visibility of Black women and girls as aspirational figures, and can inspire offline life by fueling the Black feminist imagination to think and see differently in the realm of Black women's present and future possibilities.

Nonetheless, when Linda Chavers, a disabled Black woman writer for *Elle* magazine, raised concerns about the #BlackGirlMagic hashtag, her critique was roundly dismissed by several Black women on social media. Expressing consternation about its ableist focus on Black women's *superhuman* abilities to transcend racial and sexual oppression,

Chavers writes, "Black girls and women are humans. That's all we are. And it would be a magical feeling to be treated like human beings—who can't fly, can't bounce off the ground, can't block bullets, who very much can feel pain, who very much can die" (2016). However, her critics accused her of taking the phrase too literally and for not recognizing the need for celebration of Black women's beauty and accomplishments, which are constantly scrutinized and subject to denigration.

We should not overlook Chavers's concern for the ableist rhetoric of BlackGirlMagic, however, which places undue emphasis on respectability, overachievement, and the ubiquitous "strong Black woman" that often camouflages the vulnerabilities and failures of Black women and girls. And yet, when music artist Solange Knowles—in a *Teen Vogue* interview with young actress Amandla Stenberg (who promoted the "Black Girls are Magic" T-shirt in an Instagram selfie)—described #BlackGirlMagic as "a secret language shared among Black girls who are destined to climb mountains and cross rivers in a world that tells us to belong to the valleys that surround us," she is not insisting on the "superhuman" Black girl so much as she celebrates the *transgressive* Black girl who dares to transcend her place and occupy space considered off limits. This is less about ability than it is about aspiration. As Knowles further proclaims, "Here we are . . . sprinkling black girl magic in every crevice of the universe" (2016).

Her more popular big sister Beyoncé Knowles expanded the visual vocabulary of #BlackGirlMagic with her second visual album and sixth solo effort, *Lemonade*, released in 2016. An hour-length concept album exploring the pop star's struggles with an unfaithful partner, Beyoncé intertwines the personal with the collective—situating her pain within both a historical legacy (of her ancestral mothers as well as her "daughter's daughters") and her present-day community of women (including the mothers of slain sons whose violent deaths spawned the Black Lives Matter movement). And in exploring Black women's collective resolve to not be defined by that pain, Beyoncé interconnects her artistry with poet Warsan Shire's words to conjure a *magic* born from grandmotherly wisdom:

> Grandmother, the alchemist, you spun gold out of this hard life, conjured beauty from the things left behind. Found healing where it did not live. Discovered the antidote in your own kit. Broke the curse with your own two hands. You passed these instructions down to your daughter who then passed it down to her daughter (*Lemonade*, Parkwood Entertainment, 2016 [screenplay by Warsan Shire]).

In other words, #BlackGirlMagic is about the old cliché of Black women "turning lemons into lemonade," as well as conjuring new imagery. This is evocatively shown during the "Hope" segment of the visual album featuring the song "Freedom" in which Kijafa Brown, a Black female Mardi Gras Indian crowned Queen Ya Ya of Washita Nation, circles a decorated dining room table in a mysterious ritual before we cut away to Beyoncé posing with other women covered in sacred Ori body art designed by Nigerian artist Laolu Senbajo. We also hear a voice-over uttering the word *magic* before revealing a newborn lying in the center of a bed. Here, Beyoncé shrewdly interweaves art and divinity, the black-and-white imagery invoking the ancestral past, which simultaneously ushers in a new generation. In capturing the "magical" essence of Black womanhood and girlhood, *Lemonade* becomes a mirror, as Beyoncé suggests in her acceptance speech at the 59th Grammy Awards, one that can "show images to [her] children that reflect their own beauty."

Referring to both the twins she bore and her daughter Blue Ivy, who makes several appearances throughout *Lemonade* and in the "Formation" music video, and who incidentally wore a pink tuxedo that contrasted with her mother's hyperfeminine gown at the Grammys, Beyoncé consciously connects her project of BlackGirlMagic to the next generation, even inviting a different gendered presentation on the part of Blue's outfit, which challenges the feminine expectations that have shaped the pop star's persona since her early Destiny's Child career. Nonetheless, her digitized stage performance at the Grammys, which synthesized a multiracial portrait of "Black goddess" imagery—including the Yoruba orisha Oshun, the Catholic Virgin Mary, and the Hindu goddesses Durga and Kali—literally served up the magic of a reproducing Black woman. Beyoncé's bared pregnant belly highlighted the magic of new life and the infinite possibilities of a multiplicity of Black womanhood, as reflected in the infinite mirrors duplicated on stage.

As Jordan McDonald argues, "Her continued intertwining of Black womanhood and godliness through the context of motherhood and feminine rage offers a womanist take on the matter of God" (2017). However, this *magic* is not about the creation of the Black superwoman, but instead about an album that "asserts God's distinct connection to the inner workings of Black women's lives, and doubles as a formal rejection of the pedestal Beyoncé has been offered" (McDonald 2017). This performative *magic* elevates the status of Black womanhood, even if the pop star must simultaneously proclaim, "God is God, and I am Not," these words flashing during the song "Don't Hurt Yourself" in the "Anger" segment of the visual album.

Such mediated performances have offline repercussions in which Black women are heralded for swinging elections—as occurred in the special Alabama senatorial race in 2017—or for igniting the #MeToo campaign against sexual harassment, begun by Tarana Burke and culminating in an invitation to Anita Hill to head a Hollywood-based commission against sexual harassment in the movie industry. However, there is a fine line between serving as the nation's "mammy" or "magical negro" and emerging through one's own personal Black-GirlMagic among a community of Black women and girls. The shift from online discourse and media narratives to offline action will be a critical one, as explored in the chapters of this volume, but it will have emerged because we first dreamed it, imagined it, hailed it, and magnified its possibility through the power of rhetoric and visual imagery.

Works Cited

Chavers, Linda. 2016. "Here's My Problem with #BlackGirlMagic." *Elle*. January 13. http://www.elle.com/life-love/a33180/why-i-dont-love-blackgirl magic/.

Knowles, Solange. 2016. "How Our February Cover Star Amandla Stenberg Learned to Love Her Blackness." *Teen Vogue*. January 7. http://www .teenvogue.com/story/amandla-stenberg-interview-teen-vogue-february -2016/.

McDonald, Jordan. 2017. "We Are Not Yours: Black Women Are Supreme but not Superhuman." *BitchMedia*. December 5. https://www.bitchmedia.org /article/black-women-are-not-your-personal-savior/.

Minh-ha, Trinh T. 1989. *Woman, Native, Other: Writing Postcoloniality and Feminism*. Bloomington: Indiana University Press.

ACKNOWLEDGMENTS

This book is the product of the Black women who poured their stories into the universe to guide us as we navigate race-gender structures. We are grateful for their labors.

We thank the dedicated staff at the University of Arizona Press and especially the series editors of The Feminist Wire Books: Connecting Feminisms, Race, and Social Justice, Monica J. Casper, Tamura A. Lomax, Darnell L. Moore—thanks for supporting this project. We thank the reviewers for their thoughtful comments, and to the contributing authors, thank you for trusting us with your work.

BLACK GIRL MAGIC BEYOND THE HASHTAG

WE ARE MAGIC AND WE ARE REAL

Exploring the Politics of Black Femmes, Girls,
and Women's Self-Articulation

Julia S. Jordan-Zachery and Duchess Harris

See she's telepathic
Call it black girl magic
Yeah she scares the gov'ment . . .
She don't give up
—JAMILA WOODS, "BLK GIRL SOLDIER"

Jamila Woods, in her song "Blk Girl Soldier" (2016), sings of Black-GirlMagic. But what does it mean when we, self-identified Black femmes, girls, and women, invoke BlackGirlMagic? The term *BlackGirlMagic* is used across age, class, education, and other social identity markers. But it begs the question: What *is* BlackGirlMagic? Why do Black femmes, girls, and women feel the need to consider themselves magical? What are we haunted by that is soliciting a response that asserts Black girls and women are magical? What ontological and epistemological questions does BlackGirlMagic pose? These are the questions that serve as the wellspring of this edited collection.

Black femmes, girls, and women have a long history of engaging in the politics of self-definition and self-valuation. Indeed, these politics are core principles of Black feminist thought (Collins 2000) and are reflected in Black women's literature and artistic expressions (Walker 1983). A relatively new iteration of the politics of self-definition (identity) and self-valuation (power and justice) has emerged via the hashtag #BlackGirlMagic. #BlackGirlMagic dominates social media, particularly Twitter (and Black Twitter, a community of Black-identified users within Twitter, specifically), Instagram, and Snapchat. And this hashtag travels through time and space, regardless of age and/or class.

CaShawn Thompson, who tweets at @thepbg, first used the hashtag #BlackGirlsAreMagic in 2013 as a way of articulating resistance to the invisibility—cultural, political, and social—of Black girls and women. In an interview, Thompson explains that she deployed the term *magic* because "it's something that people don't always understand. . . . Sometimes our [Black women's] accomplishments might seem to come out of thin air, because a lot of times, the only people supporting us are other Black women" (quoted in Thomas, 2015). But even before Thompson's creation of a hashtagged iteration of BlackGirlMagic, the understading of Black women's use of *magic* was articulated. As early as 1983, Alice Walker used the concept of magic to describe the work done by Black women, a historical antecedent that we, the editors, explore.

Since Thompson's initial use of #BlackGirlsAreMagic, the hashtag and the concept have gained such popularity that Thompson now refers to them as a "movement." In *Black Girl Magic Beyond the Hashtag: Twenty-First-Century Acts of Self-Definition* we take up the meaning of BlackGirlMagic, a political and cultural statement, by asking: How does BlackGirlMagic translate outside of social media? More specifically, this collected volume addresses a larger question, namely: How do Black femmes, girls, and women make meaning of their identity(ies) and social locations in a neoliberal context that can, at times, make them "disappear"?

Black Girl Magic Beyond the Hashtag is an edited volume that investigates Black femmes', girls', and women's self-articulation and space-making—culturally and politically. At its core, it is an exploration of Black gendered identity and how Black femmes, girls, and women make meaning of their lives in a context of the very public display of Black death (Sandra Bland, for example) and resistance to such state and/or quasi-state-sanctioned murders. Each chapter interrogates the history of this naming process, using different contexts and cases, by placing #BlackGirlMagic—the iconography of it—in conversation with other moments of Black femmes', girls', and women's self-naming and self-evaluation. Informed by Black feminist intersectionality theory, among other theories, the chapters comprising this edited volume explore a multiplicity of Black femmes', girls', and women's praxis and behaviors.

As we conceptualized this collection, we were committed to a set of chapters that were interdisciplinary, and that utilized myriad approaches to understanding the multidimensionality of Black girlhood and womanhood. These two elements undergird our organization of this edited volume because of our commitment, as researchers who are also Black women and who are raising Black girls, to advancing feminist research across disciplines and to pushing the boundaries of Black feminist thought. As such, each author, in their own way, presents a critical articulation of Black femmes', girls', and women's subjectivity that works to bridge the academy and community.

As the Jamaican-born cultural theorist and activist Stuart Hall (1982) asserts, the introduction of new terms offers an opportunity to ask a new set of questions, to see old questions (and problems) in new ways, and to organize and theorize knowledge and experiences in new ways, thereby enabling new discursive and praxis interventions. We do not pretend to offer a definitive explanation of the notion of BlackGirlMagic; instead, we view this collection as part of the litany of Black women's actions designed to bring us to the center—as research subjects and critical political and cultural consumers, but more importantly, as producers of knowledge based on their/our sense of being. We situate our interrogations into BlackGirlMagic based on the notion that Black femmes, girls, and women theorize based on their "constructions, history, and real life experiences" (Bobo 1995, 310), and not only in the sense of how the academy understands the production of knowledge.

Black Girl Magic Beyond the Hashtag provides a much-needed context for exploring recent developments in Black femmes', girls', and women's studies. By centering the complexity of *magic* and its intersection with the lived realities of Black girlhood and womanhood, this volume highlights what Black feminist scholars and others identify as the three tenets of Black political and cultural behaviors—identity, power, and justice (Jordan-Zachery and Alexander Floyd 2018; Brown 2009; Cooper 1995; Collins 2000; hooks 1990). We posit that #BlackGirlMagic is but one manifestation of Black women's political and cultural behaviors, and, as such, embodies the three tenets articulated by Black feminist scholars and activists.

How these tenets are articulated, vis-à-vis #BlackGirlMagic, is captured in four elements: (1) community building and making, as BlackGirlMagic serves as a form of intracommunication methodology; (2) challenging dehumanizing representations via a practice of self-definition; (3) rendering Black femmes, girls, and women visible; and (4) restoring what is sometimes violently taken. These are the common themes that are identified in the chapters that comprise this volume, and that constitute the substance of #BlackGirlMagic. These elements may be different and/or similar to other articulations of Black women's political and cultural behaviors.

These four elements that constitute #BlackGirlMagic are embodied and enacted both on and offline. They afford Black femmes, girls, and women the opportunity to engage in a practice, vis-à-vis #BlackGirlMagic, to make whole from fragments (that result from race-gender oppressive structures), exist in a space that is neither sacred nor secular, and deploy speculative freedom. These practices were identified, primarily, via our critical readings of the chapters in this volume.

This introduction notes the conceptual and epistemological challenges and opportunities presented by the articulation of BlackGirlMagic. We start with a brief review of the complex realities faced by Black femmes, girls, and women, primarily within the context of the United States. This is then followed by an exploration of the evolution of BlackGirlMagic.

Complex Lived Realties

Globally, Black femmes, girls, and women face complex lived realities as a result of gendered-raced-classed-sexuality oppressions. While this edited volume is not primarily focused on the results and impacts of these oppressions, we want to pause ever so briefly to highlight a few impacts to show a part of the context within which BlackGirlMagic emerged. We recognize that this small reflection is not historical and does not fully capture the depth of the impact of oppressions. Furthermore, we acknowledge that not all Black femmes, girls, and women experience these oppressions in the same way, as some have differential access to resources.

Black femmes, girls, and women tend to be disproportionately disadvantaged economically, physically, educationally, and socially. These experiences vary from individual to individual, and are often reflective of a particular context, such as geography and other factors that influence or impact lived experiences. In light of not finding one source with comparable data that allow us to paint a picture of diasporic Black women, we opted to center the United Nations Entity for Gender Equality and the Empowerment of Women's (UN Women 2018) most recent report and then offer more detailed information on Black girls and women in the United States by looking specifically at variables such as access to income, wealth and employment, health and well-being, and educational access.

Access to Income, Wealth, and Employment

Gender inequality often results in women and girls disproportionately experiencing poverty regardless of their geographic location. According to the UN Women (2018) report, in Latin America and the Caribbean, women aged twenty-five to thirty-four experience extreme poverty—there are 132 women living in extreme poverty for every one hundred men. Regarding sub-Saharan Africa,[1] the UN says that there are 127 women aged twenty-five to thirty-four living in extreme poverty for every one hundred men. Black girls and women in the United States also find themselves represented disproportionately among the poor. Consider that while 62 percent of Black women are actively participating in the labor force, their median annual earnings ($34,000) are less than "most women's and men's earning" (DuMonthier, Childers, and Milli 2017). As a result, 24.6 percent of Black women in the United States live in poverty compared to 10.8 percent of white women and 18.9 percent of Black men (DuMonthier, Childers, and Milli 2017). Black girls also experience poverty at alarming rates. In 2014, it was estimated that almost 40 percent of Black females under the age of eighteen lived in poverty (*Black Demographics* n.d.).

Health and Overall Well-Being

There is much to focus on regarding Black femmes,' girls,' and women's health and overall well-being. We offer a snapshot of violence—interpartner; what Epstein, Blake, and González (2017) refer to as the "adultification" of Black girls in the United States; and maternal death and/or infant mortality rates. In Latin America and the Caribbean, among girls and women aged fifteen to forty-nine, 21 percent reported an experience of interpartner physical and/or sexual violence within a twelve-month period. Within that same time frame, 22.3 percent of women and girls in sub-Saharan Africa, of the same age range, reported intimate partner violence (UN Women 2018). While not comparable data, in the United States it is reported that 40 percent of Black women, within their lifetimes, experienced intimate partner violence (DuMonthier, Childers, and Milli 2017).

Violence against Black femmes, girls, and women is not limited to the domestic sphere. Recently, attention has been paid to Black girls in the United States and how they experience violence vis-à-vis the school system. Epstein, Blake, and González show that the adultification of Black girls helps to explain how school systems inflict violence on Black girls through disciplinary actions such as suspensions, thereby robbing them of their childhood. As they argue, "Given established discrepancies in law enforcement and juvenile court practices that disproportionately affect Black girls, the perception of Black girls as less innocent and more adult-like may contribute to *more punitive exercise of discretion* by those in positions of authority, *greater use of force, and harsher penalties*" (2017, 1; emphasis added).

Beyond the experience of such forms of violence, which impact the well-being of Black femmes, girls, and women, there is also the experience of disproportionately high maternal deaths among this population. As reported, the maternal mortality ratio (MMR) in sub-Saharan Africa is among the highest, with 556 deaths per one hundred thousand live births. In Latin America and the Caribbean, there were sixty-eight maternal deaths per one hundred thousand live births in 2015, which is lower than the global average of 216. It is estimated that in the United States, "Black women are more than three times as likely to die due to pregnancy and childbirth as White women (42.8 deaths per 100,000 live births for Black women versus 12.5 deaths per 100,000 live births for White women)" (DuMonthier, Childers, and Milli 2017, 97).

Educational Access

According to the UN Women's (2018) report, "15 million girls of primary school age will never get the chance to learn to read or write in primary school, compared to 10 million boys." With regard to adolescent girls in sub-Saharan Africa, it is estimated that 48.1 percent of girls, compared to 43.6 percent of boys, are out of school (UN Women 2018). Simultaneously, Black girls in the United States are experiencing their own set of challenges within the education system. Between 2011 and 2012, 45 percent of Black girls in grades K–12 were suspended from school (DuMonthier, Childers, and Milli 2017, 120). Monique W. Morris (2016) speaks to how Black girls are systematically pushed out of school and the long-term implications for such race-gender policing of Black girls in school. What she shows is that the impacts cover a wide spectrum: academic, social, and emotional.

At the same time, Black femmes and women in the United States have registered improvements in higher education. Between 2004 and 2014, the share of Black women with a bachelor's degree or higher increased by 23.9 percent, making Black women the group of women with the second-largest improvement in attainment of higher education during the decade (DuMonthier, Childers, and Milli 2017, xix). The dichotomy is that while Black women's access to higher education and degree attainment have increased, the benefits, in terms of economic mobility, have not increased commensurately. As Asha DuMonthier, Chandra Childers, and Jessica Milli (2017) indicate, Black women face "continued high unemployment, low earnings, and concentration in occupations that offer few benefits, [leaving] many facing economic instability and inadequate access to resources and opportunities" (65).

Black femmes, girls, and women—regardless of social or physical location—encounter structural violence. As described by Paul Farmer et al. (2006),

Structural violence is one way of describing social arrangements that put individuals and populations in harm's way. . . . The arrangements are structural because they are embedded in the political and economic organization of our social world; they are violent because they cause injury to people. . . . [N]either culture nor pure individual will is at fault; rather, historically given (and often economically driven) processes and forces conspire to constrain individual agency. Structural violence is visited upon all those whose social status denies them access to the fruits of scientific and social progress.

Such violence has a wide-ranging impact—economic, education, and health, among others—that travels through time and space, and, as such, can serve to limit Black femmes', girls', and women's well-being. BlackGirlMagic may be understood, in part, as a response to such structural violence and the labor that Black femmes, girls, and women undertake to exist, survive, and thrive.

It's Magic, Gurl

There is no single identity used by Black femmes, girls, and women; however, the tie that binds them across time and space is their efforts to liberate Black femmes, girls, women, and other oppressed groups from economic, social, health, housing, criminal justice, and cultural inequalities. Research, whether in history, political science, or sociology, has sought to understand and explain the processes and politics of Black femmes', girls', and women's self-articulation and self-valuation by the mutually constitutive forces that shape Black femmes', girls', and women's lived realities.

Despite this growing body of research, there are too few studies that center the voices of Black femmes, girls, and women (though, at the same time, we recognize that some disciplines are better represented than others). The history of Black women's self-articulation is not a new phenomenon. As Barbara Smith, the founder of the Combahee River Collective, stated,

> I think we came up with the term "identity politics." I never really saw it anywhere else and I would suggest that people, if they really want to find the origin of the term, that they try to find it in any place earlier than in the Combahee River Collective statement. I don't remember seeing it anywhere else. But what we meant by identity politics was a politics that grew out of our objective material experiences as Black women. This was the kind of politics that had never been done or practiced before to our knowledge, although we began to find out that there were Black feminists in the early part of this century and also, perhaps, in the latter part of the nineteenth century. But it had never been quite formulated in the way that we were trying to formulate it, particularly because we were talking about homophobia, lesbian identity, as well. (quoted in Harris 2018, 130)

Smith suggested, and rightly so, that there is a long history of Black women's efforts to name their experiences in a manner that is unique and representative of them, and in a manner that is inclusive of difference. Years after the publication of the Combahee River Collective statement, there remain many areas related to Black femmes, girls, and women that are understudied, and there exists a dearth of interdisciplinary research. Thus, we are left with the question: How do Black femmes, girls, and women render themselves visible in structures that oppress and construct them as invisible or hypervisible? *Black Girl Magic Beyond the Hashtag*, via an interdisciplinary lens, addresses this larger question.

#BlackGirlMagic, although used widely in the digital world, is a term begging definition and some form of operationalization. We make this claim, not in a positivist or even postpositivist academic sense. Nor do we make this claim to necessarily collapse the concept into a singular understanding. Rather, it is our intention to better understand what makes Black femmes, girls, and women *magical*. When and how do we know that *magic* is the cause of their success? Furthermore, how do we create a context within which *magic* might materialize?

Collectively, the volume bridges theory and practice by offering critical interventions that speak to contexts that allow Black femmes, girls, and women to thrive and flourish, and show us how magic manifests in the everyday actions of Black femmes, girls, and women. #BlackGirlMagic *offline* not only explores questions about the performance of identity, as well as the politics of interlocking parts of one's identity—race, class, gender, sexuality, and representation—but also offers critical insights into fostering a radical performance of Black girlhood and womanhood that allows us to bridge the academy, the community, and the digital and offline worlds as a means of supporting Black femmes', girls', and women's quests for freedom. This is one way that #BlackGirlMagic asserts power, even offline.

In her book *In Search of Our Mothers' Gardens*, Alice Walker writes of the (Black) women who were "driven to a numb and bleeding madness by the springs of creativity in them for which there was no release, and I knew I did not want to be one of those women. They were creators who lived lives of spiritual waste" (1983, 233). Walker also suggested that despite oppressive race, gender, and class structures, these same women "handed on the creative spark, the seed of a flower they themselves never hoped to see: or like a sealed letter they could not plainly read" (240). This speaks to a form of prefigurative *politics* and a sensibility of self, whereby Black women imagine and create a "universe in the image of her personal conception of Beauty" (241) by utilizing whatever space she found herself in and seemed to grow "as if by magic." Black women, Walker continued, planted gardens "brilliant with colors" while making "all the clothes that we wore" and "all the towels that we used" (241, 238). What Walker's work suggests, in part, is that Black women work to manifest their visions of themselves.

Toni Morrison also prefigured the notion of the "magical" Black woman. In a 1988 interview, Morrison said,

> My own use of enchantment simply comes because that's the way the world was for me and for the black people that I knew. In addition to the very shrewd, down-to-earth, efficient way in which they did things and survived things, there was this other knowledge or perception, always discredited but nevertheless there, which informed their sensibilities and clarified their activities. It formed a kind of cosmology that was perceptive as well as enchanting, and so it seemed impossible for me to write about black people and eliminate that simply because it was "unbelievable." (quoted in Davis 1988, 144)

In speaking of magic and Black girlhood and/or womanhood, Black women such as Walker, Morrison, and Thompson are not necessarily speaking of hocus-pocus. Instead, they are explaining an ideology, belief, or practice that allows Black femmes, girls, and women to exist within an oppressive system. Using all of these sources as our point of departure, below, we offer key components of the notion of Black-GirlMagic. What we argue is that #BlackGirlMagic is a form of critical literacy used by Black femmes, girls, and women as they work to invent and/or imagine themselves in a society that often renders them invisible or hypervisible and subjects them and their communities to illicit violence. We now turn our attention to the elements that constitute #BlackGirlMagic.

Intracommunication Methodology

The term *girl* is part of the functioning of the critical literacy of #BlackGirlMagic, and it serves as a means of intragroup communi-

cation. So how do we understand the term *girl*, especially in relation
to the *community-building* work that it performs for Black femmes,
girls, and women? While we are primarily focused on how *girl* functions as a means for community building, we must address the issue
of age. Cox argues that the field of girlhood studies challenges the
"changing nature of citizenship for young women who are defined
primarily by their status as both female and adults in the making"
(2015, 12). As we posit, #BlackGirlMagic recognizes this understanding of girlhood, but it is not bound by chronological age or society's
conceptualization of moving into adulthood. Instead, the term, often
deployed colloquially as "gurl," "homegirl," "sista-girl," etc., represents
a way of acknowledging commonalities among Black femmes, girls,
and women. Thus, we argue that the use of the term *girl* is more in
line with the definition offered by Ruth Nicole Brown, who defines
girlhood, in her book *Hear Our Truths*, as "a political articulation that
intentionally points to Black girls . . . beyond those who identify and
are identified as Black girls" (2013, 7). Furthermore, Brown defines
Black girlhood as "the representations, memories, and lived experiences of being and becoming in a body marked as youthful, Black,
and female. Black girlhood is not dependent, then, on age, physical
maturity, or any essential category of identity" (2009, 1).

As we understand the term *girl*, it is not dependent on age, physical maturity, or indeed *any* category of identity for it to serve as a
method for community building that encourages and/or promotes
communication or expression of self, both individual and collective.
In this sense, the use of the term *girl* defies social categorization and
the boundaries that often result from such. The fluidity embedded in
the term *girl* is an important aspect of #BlackGirlMagic.

The term *girl*, which embodies race and gender (and other identity markers), also offers an intracommunication methodology. Such
expressions, like *girl*, are often used as part of the call-and-response
mechanisms used by Black femmes, girls, and women to suggest

relatedness to one another. It is also a practice of resistance. In this sense, *girl* is read as a performance of the intersection of race and gender (and other identity markers) and works as a form of "kinetic orality" (West 1989), which is a form of metacommunication. In defining kinetic orality, Cornel West states,

> The concrete, everyday response to institutionalized terrorism—slavery or Jim-Crowism—was to deploy weapons of kinetic orality, passionate physicality, and combative spirituality to survive and dream of freedom. By kinetic orality, I mean dynamic repetitive and energetic rhetorical styles that form communities, e.g., antiphonal styles and linguistic innovations that accent fluid, improvisational identities. By passionate physicality, I mean bodily stylizations of the world, syncopations and polyrhythms that assert one's somebodiness in a society in which one's body has no public worth, only economic value as a laboring metabolism. And by combative spirituality, I mean a sense of historical patience, subversive joy, and daily perseverance in an apparently hopeless and meaningless historical situation. (1989, 93)

Thus, *girl* becomes important in this practice of "kinetic orality"— what Gaunt calls "in-body formula" through which a Black musical identity is "subjectively embodied" and "communally performed" (2006, 70). In this sense, *girl* works to bind Black *femaleness*, regardless of whether or not this category was assigned at birth, across the aesthetic thought of as *magic*. By no means are we suggesting that there is a flattening out of differences that equates Black girlhood and womanhood. Although the term is used across age and maturation, the performance of #BlackGirlMagic provides space, because it is communally performed, for self-identified Black females to express their multidimensional and varied lived experiences.

Blackness is an integral part of the sisterhood of BlackGirlMagic because race cannot be extracted from the formula. In times when the solidarity of sisterhood should be enough for all women, specific instances in history prove that Black femmes, girls, and women often use their magic to take care of themselves because their needs are not a priority for the rest of the world. Indeed, they are often not even *considered*. #BlackGirlMagic is a means of resistance and insistence in a white feminist-dominated landscape where the primary means of resistance is "leaning in" (Sandberg 2013). How much more could Black girls, femmes, and women lean in without falling over?

In this collection, our authors' emphasis is on the perseverance of Black femmes, girls, and women who have maintained their humanity in the face of hostility. During a 2016 acceptance speech for the BET Humanitarian Award, actor and activist Jesse Williams articulated this idea in an impassioned discourse about race in the United States. The speech ended with a subtle nod that some may not have recognized:

> The burden of the brutalized is not to comfort the bystander. That's not our job, alright—stop with all that. If you have a critique for the resistance, for our resistance, then you better have an established record of critique of our oppression. If you have no interest, if you have no interest in equal rights for black people, then do not make suggestions to those who do. Sit down. We've been floating this country on credit for centuries, yo, and we're done watching and waiting while this invention called whiteness uses and abuses us, burying black people out of sight and out of mind while extracting our culture, our dollars, our entertainment like oil—black gold, ghettoizing and demeaning our creations, then stealing them, gentrifying our genius, and trying us on like costumes before discarding our bodies like rinds of strange fruit. *The thing is though . . . the thing is that just because we're magic doesn't mean we're not real.* (Williams 2016, emphasis added)

Williams was respectfully referencing the #BlackGirlMagic movement, alluding to the fact that #BlackGirlMagic serves as a restorative reminder that within Black femme, girl, and women identities there is resistance to dominant narratives and a willingness of these femmes, girls, and women to define themselves for themselves.

Self-Definition

Beyond an attempt to foster a community in the face of oppressive structures, #BlackGirlMagic also signifies a tool used by Black femmes, girls, and women to challenge dehumanizing representations by tapping into the power of self-definition. According to Patricia Hill Collins, "Self-definition is the quest to move from silence to language to individual and group action" (2000, 120). This is the type of self-definition spoken of by Cox in *Shapeshifters: Black Girls and the Choreography of Citizenship* (2015) and Ruth Nicole Brown in *Hear Our Truths* (2013). Cox speaks to "choreography" used by Black girls as a way of "theorizing" how they use their bodies to alter spaces, thereby making room for themselves, individually and collectively, as they confront various oppressions. These girls engage in shapeshifting, which serves as a form of self-expression that, in turn, according to Cox, is inherently political. Brown's work, with the group she co-created called Saving Our Lives Hear Our Truths (SOLHOT), also shows how girls and women involved in this group work make meaning and bring to life a vision of themselves that is defined by themselves. She argues that the performances of SOLHOT "enable the affirmation of the particulars of lived experiences" (Brown 2013, 14). She further argues that Black girls (femmes and women) need to carve out spaces for representation in service of themselves because "narratives created about Black girls without our input never seem to recognize our worth, value, and our power" (Brown 2009, 1–2).

The varied representations of #BlackGirlMagic, as curated in digital spaces, afford Black girls and women the opportunity to engage in expressions of self-articulation. As Jordan-Zachery states, "Black women's bodies are sites through which knowledge about race, class, sexuality and gender and their intersections are structured" (2017, 28). The communicative potential of visual images of Black girls and women that often accompany #BlackGirlMagic on Twitter and Instagram allows for an exploration of the complex interplay of race, gender, power, and identity (see Wilson 2003) vis-à-vis how Black femmes, girls, and women choose to represent their bodies and their experiences. This type of self-articulation and digital curation of experiences are also reflected in #BlackGirlJoy, #CareFreeBlackGirl, and #BlackWomenAtWork, the latter of which was used to bring to light the race-gender oppression faced by Black women in the workforce (McGirt 2017). Black femmes, girls, and women, through hashtags, are engaged in a form of radical curation, which "is the use of curatorial practices to present, with care, a themed collection of art(efacts) that represent oft-unheard and sometimes disruptive chronicles or groups" (El-Hadi 2015). The femmes, girls, and women who engage in #BlackGirlMagic seek to create and maintain a sphere of freedom for Black femmes', girls', and women's social and political discourses. And they do this, in part, by controlling the presentation of their bodies, because, as Kelly asserts, "the social and cultural world is always embodied, its meanings are carried on the body, which is, itself, a social and cultural site of struggle within and against this social order" (1997, 102).

A new and growing body of literature, Black feminist visual culture and theory, seeks to blur the boundaries between the subject and object dyad by repositioning Black women as not simply the objects of art but, instead, as embodying a subject position. Black feminist visual culture analyzes and chronicles African American women's, and others', ways of resistance across various visual practices (see, for example, Brown 2015). In *Picture Freedom*, Jasmine Nichole Cobb (2015) shows how formerly enslaved individuals rejected notions of the gaze, thereby rejecting "othering," and, in turn, gazed back at the

viewer. While we are hesitant to offer an all-encompasing categorization of this body of literature, we suggest that a common thread is
that it offers a meaningful and useful theory of representation. Nash
asks us to consider "how representation can be a site where specta-
tors and protagonists exercise freedom even within the confines of a
visual field structured by race and gender" (2014, 6). What this suggests is that Black femmes, girls, and women, as "performers," can
be simultaneously influenced by oppressive structures and, in turn,
influence oppressive structures by exercising agency in terms of how
they represent themselves within these structures—even if there are
limitations on how they are able to exercise agency (see Gaunt 2006).
Through the use of #BlackGirlMagic, Black femmes, girls, and women
are resisting dominant norms of Black girlhood and womanhood,
and are instead engaging in the actions theorized by Black feminists
that seek a radical democratic practice by claiming space for their
articulations of self. #BlackGirlMagic allows Black femmes, girls, and
women the opportunity to create new iconographies via a process of
reimagination, so that that they can present to the world the picture
that represents them.

Making Self and (In)Justice Visible

Additionally, #BlackGirlMagic represents an effort to make Black
femmes, girls, and women visible. Simply put, Black femmes, girls,
and women go missing—physically, emotionally, and culturally.
In their 2010 study, Sesko and Biernat show how Black women go
unnoticed and their voices go unheard. But Black femmes, girls, and
women have long known how society works to render them invisible. Consider that in 1833 Mariah Stewart said, "Men of eminence
have mostly risen from obscurity; nor will I, although a female of a
darker hue, and far more obscure than they, bend my head or hand

my harp upon willows; for though poor, I will virtuous prove" (quoted in Richardson 1987, 45). Years later, Kimberlé Crenshaw, executive director of the African American Policy Forum (AAPF), explained the hashtag #SayHerName by saying, "Although Black women are routinely killed, raped, and beaten by the police, their experiences are rarely foregrounded in popular understandings of police brutality. Yet, inclusion of Black women's experiences in social movements, media narratives, and policy demands around policing and police brutality is critical to effectively combatting racialized state violence for Black communities and other communities of color" (Crenshaw et al. 2015). Invisibility has long haunted Black femmes, girls and women, and, as such, their practices—political, cultural, and economic—have often centered on making themselves visible. They make themselves visible to not only highlight injustices but to offer a vision of justice, one based on their lived experiences. This is exactly what Thompson was alluding to when she offered her explanation of #BlackGirlMagic and its widespread use.

#BlackGirlMagic offers a critique of both historical and contemporary representations of Black femmes, girls, and women that include invisibility and hypervisibility that are often marked on their bodies. Invisibility and hypervisibility are marked on Black women's bodies via scripts (Jordan-Zachery 2017). Jordan-Zachery offers two dominant scripts that are often written onto Black women's, femmes', and girls' bodies: *The Ass* and *Strong Black Woman* scripts. As Jordan-Zachery posits, "Scripting, which provides a means for understanding, projecting meanings, and categorizing, is an integral part of the marginalization of Black women, as it influences how groups (both in- and out-groups) interact with Black women" (2017, 33).

As Gabrielle Union's character Mary Jane Paul so poignantly stated in the television show *Being Mary Jane*, "Black women aren't ugly, they are invisible" (Graham, Quinn, and Akil 2015). #BlackGirlMagic is a part of Union's assertion to make Black femmes, girls, and women visible. Black femmes, girls, and women, as a way of countering the invisibility they face, use hashtags such as #BlackGirlMagic and #BlackGirlJoy, among others. They do this on multiple social media platforms, including, especially, Twitter, and a community on the platform that is referred to as Black Twitter. In describing Black Twitter, Soraya Nadia McDonald states, "Perhaps the most significant contribution of Black Twitter is that it increases visibility of black people online, and in doing so, dismantles the idea that white is standard and everything else is 'other.' It's a radical demand for acceptance by simply existing—or sometimes dominating—in a space and being yourself, without apology or explanation" (2014). Hashtags are a way of countering invisibility as they can serve as a means for personal and social consciousness-raising and social organizing. They insert the user into the public marketplace of ideas.

#BlackGirlMagic also seeks to restore that which is sometimes violently taken from Black femmes, girls, and women. Consider that #BlackLivesMatter served as one of the first mainstream national and global hashtags used to bring attention to state, quasi-state, and private violence directed toward Black individuals in the United States. Additionally, as referenced above, #SayHerName, coined by AAPF in February 2015, represents the movement to center the stories of Black femmes, girls, and women, and call attention to their experiences with state-sanctioned violence.

These hashtags have been used digitally and in the real world as a way of resisting Black death and claiming Black humanity. Manuel Castells, whose work examines internet studies and social movements, suggests hashtags and hashtag activism serve to create community, in the sense that they create a public space for deliberation, "which ultimately becomes a political space, a space for sovereign assemblies to meet and to recover their rights of representation" (2015, 152). Alicia

Garza, one of the founders of #BlackLivesMatter, speaks to how the hashtag moved offline, embodying community and representation:

> We were humbled when cultural workers, artists, designers, and techies offered their labor and love to expand #BlackLivesMatter beyond a social media hashtag. Opal, Patrisse, and I created the infrastructure for this movement project—moving the hashtag from social media to the streets. Our team grew through a very successful Black Lives Matter ride, led and designed by Patrisse Cullors and Darnell L. Moore, organized to support the movement that is growing in St. Louis, MO, after 18-year old Mike Brown was killed at the hands of Ferguson Police Officer Darren Wilson. We've hosted national conference calls focused on issues of critical importance to Black people working hard for the liberation of our people. We've connected people across the country working to end the various forms of injustice impacting our people. We've created space for the celebration and humanization of Black lives. (2014)

The various movements—cultural, political, or both (and sometimes the distinctions are, blurred as Zachery and Jordan-Zachery, in this volume, articulate)—and the hashtags, created and curated by diverse Black femmes, girls, and women, serve to (re)write dominant narratives in which Black femmes, girls, and women tend to be ignored in larger public discussions, including, but not limited to, state violence. In this instance, #BlackGirlMagic serves to assert a type of power by telling the story of Black femmes, girls, and women in their own language and style. Whether used offline, online, or in combination, these self-representations hint at transgressive possibilities that are grounded in the realities of Black femmes, girls, and women. They represent a practice of reclaiming what is often violently taken—a sense of self—from Black femmes, girls, and women.

Restoration

Finally, #BlackGirlMagic creates space for freedom by offering an alternative temporality that imagines a different present and future for Black femmes, girls, and women. For example, consider #Black-GirlsareFromtheFuture, created by Renina Jarmon. Jarmon, in thinking through the meaning and significance of the hashtag, asserted, "#BlackGirlsareFromtheFuture because we make the shit we believe in" (quoted in Dionne 2013). This alternative temporality is expressed through Black femmes', girls', and women's verbal and other aesthetic presentations. According to Brown, verbal styles, of which #BlackGirlMagic is one, contribute "to conversations that direct our attention to the fullness of a visionary Black girlhood as a space of freedom" (2013, 14). Black femmes, girls, and women have deployed #BlackGirlMagic to construct their "legibility as fully human" (Cox 2015, 10). Via the use of the hashtag, Black femmes, girls, and women are engaged in a project that enables them to communicate in a vibrant (and alternative) creative language that articulates their understanding of their lived experiences and (in some instances) an understanding of social justice. Through these various hashtags, and offline iterations of the ideas embodied by the hashtag, Black femmes, girls, and women are claiming a past, critiquing a present, and organizing a future where they are seen and where they reject the violence they experience—by doing the work Walker speaks about in *In Search of Our Mothers' Gardens*. They are creating, they are working, and they are resisting.

Unearthing Magic: Themes of the Chapters

Since introduced by Thompson in 2013, the term #BlackGirlMagic has been used widely, and has become part of the lexicon of digital Blackness. To some extent, it has also become commodified (for example, by the selling of T-shirts and other merchandise). While the notion of BlackGirlMagic spreads in cyberspace and other places, the question remains: How is BlackGirlMagic experienced offline? The chapters that comprise this volume address this question. They move us beyond social media's visual representations by offering analyses of the lived experiences of Black femmes, girls, and women, and how they negotiate the politics of invisibility through intracommunication methodologies in their efforts to arrive at self-definition and self-valuation and restoration. The chapters herein speak to how Black girls and women foster community, counter invisibility, engage in restorative acts, and create spaces for freedom. In essence, they show how Black femmes, girls, and women practice #BlackGirlMagic.

The analyses of the volume, to borrow from Nikol G. Alexander-Floyd (2012), consider #BlackGirlMagic to be both an idea and an ideography. As an idea, #BlackGirlMagic, similar to the concept of intersectionality, describes the intersection of oppressive structures—racism, classism, and sexism, among others (Crenshaw 1989)—that are confronted by Black femmes, girls, and women and how they resist these structures. Regarding #BlackGirlMagic as an ideography, we understand it as a term, used outside of the academy, that seeks to examine and challenge the invisibility resulting from oppressive forces faced by Black femmes, girls, and women.

Thus, as an ideography, #BlackGirlMagic is designed to capture and theorize what and how Black femmes, girls, and women do to achieve justice. By considering #BlackGirlMagic as an idea and an ideography, we are better positioned to understand how Black femmes, girls, and women perform *magic*. What the collection shows is that the labor required for success is not magical. It is real, and this labor can—and almost always does—exact a cost from those who might appear magical.

Deploying various qualitative approaches to unmask the essence of Black femmes', girls', and women's perseverance against oppressive structures, the chapters in this volume paint a picture of the *magic* used by Black femmes, girls, and women. As they fight for recognition, and as they persevere against oppressive structures, the chapters show how the magic displayed in digital spaces such as Twitter is a combination of joy, pain, hope, fulfillment, anger, disillusionment, fatigue, and a commitment to justice and freedom. Throughout the book, the analyses show that *magic* is an actual skillset that undergirds Black girls' and women's functioning "within, yet beyond, the demands of dominant ideology" (Sandoval 2000, 44). The term invokes how Black femmes, girls, and women live on the margins while also being insiders. It simultaneously emphasizes cultural specificity and difference, oppression and liberation. In a sense, #BlackGirlMagic is a mixture of the objective and the subjective. Additionally, it is both a discourse and a performance. #BlackGirlMagic can be read as a political, cultural, and historical interpretation of Black femmes', girls', and women's lives in relation, directly and indirectly, to Western philosophic thought. If read in this manner, #BlackGirlMagic is a form of resistance. The assertion of #BlackGirlMagic seeks to establish truth, order, and reality as understood from Black femmes', girls', and women's perspectives. Below, we explore the themes that cut across the various chapters of this volume—these are themes that embody our theorization of the four elements of #BlackGirlMagic: intracommunication methodology, challenging dehumanizing representations, rendering themselves visible, and practicing restoration. As we show, the overarching themes include: making a whole from fragments, neither sacred nor secular, and speculative freedom.

Making a Whole from Fragments

One of the real labors that is a part of BlackGirlMagic is reassembling the fragments that often constitute Black girls', femmes', and women's lived realities. It is Black women's struggles against "the shadow of neoliberalism, post-racialism" (David, this volume) and systemic violence that produce these fragments. The notion of Black femmes, girls, and women making a whole from fragments runs throughout the volume. So, what are the fragments that Black women are using to construct a whole? And, more importantly, how are they laboring to achieve wholeness? Charlotte E. Jacobs writes, "In the social arena, the overall experience for Black girls is a narrative of constantly trying to fit into a school culture that was not made for them" (this volume). Her words capture what we understand as fragments. The fragments are the reality confronted by Black femmes, girls, and women, globally, that captures how they are citizens but are never afforded the full benefits and protections of citizenship, how they belong but are often relegated to the margins, and how they are expected to labor for others while denying their needs. Fragments result from the legacy of colonial practices and resulting migration as shown in the chapters by Rashida L. Harrison and Leconte J. Dill et al.

In the words of Jessica L. Robinson (this volume) Black femmes, girls, and women engage in a "particular kind of laboring" in an attempt to make a whole. Black femmes, girls, and women are often expected to labor in service of others—to make other people's fragments into a whole. Zora Neal Hurston, in *Their Eyes Were Watching God*, captures this when she writes, "De nigger woman is de mule uh de world so fur as Ah can see" (1990, 14). The chapters that make up this volume show how Black femmes, girls, and women are rejecting this appropriation of their labor and demonstrate how they engage in a "cohesive organized resistance" (Harrison, this volume). They are indeed ploughing (symbolically) their own fields.

Making a whole of fragments is poignantly captured in Porshé R. Garner's chapter, "What We Know and How We Know It? Defining Black Girlhood Spirituality." In this chapter, Garner demonstrates how, in part through the teachings of her grandmother, she works to create spaces that "enact liberatory Black girlhood" by tapping into the "power that exists within"—this is the *magic*. In "Conjuring Ghosts:

Black Girlhood Hauntings and Speculative Performances of Reappearances," Jessica L. Robinson shows how she made Kasandra (Kasi) Perkins (who was murdered by her partner, Jovan Belcher) "appear" through the act of knowing and remembering. It was through her speculative performance, "Kasi to her Homegirls," that Robinson was able to move "the knowing and remembering to an embodied experience that allows for not just what is seen to be knowledge but what is felt and heard to be considered knowledge as well." She made Perkins whole and not just a victim of domestic violence at the hands of her famous boyfriend. She stripped away some of the dominant narratives that tend to disappear or treat women such as Perkins as suspect. Through her labor, others were able to see her humanity.

In making a whole out of fragments—fragments that result from race-gender-class-heteronormative neoliberal practices and structures—looking back, reimagining the present, and imagining a future centered on liberation become key. As Charlotte E. Jacobs states, "Black girls use particular competencies to recognize, process, and respond to messages that they receive connected to their status as Black adolescent girls in U.S. society while simultaneously crafting their own sense of their Black girl identities" (this volume).

The notion of fragments is also taken up in Marlo D. David's visual analysis of the hair styling aesthetics of Black women and femmes who participate in and/or identify with Afropunk. She opens her chapter with the story of Brooklyn-based musician Tamar-Kali Brown, who details how she asserted her identity around diasporic Blackness and punk culture. Brown details how she merges "her punk aesthetics to African adornment practices" in a manner that allows her to exist in a space that is often read as not a place for Black women or femmes. She, like the other Black women and femmes analyzed by David, make a whole of fragments to create their own identity and/or identities within punk culture, thereby expressing their understanding of magic.

The various authors chart this journey by situating Black femmes', girls', and women's lived experiences in the vein suggested by bell hooks, for example. According to hooks, Black women's

> lived experience may shape our consciousness in such a way that our world view differs from those who have a degree of privilege (however relative within the existing system). It is essential for continued feminist struggle that black women recognize the special vantage point our marginality gives us and make use of this perspective to criticize the dominant racist, classist, sexist hegemony as well as to envision and create a counter-hegemony. (1984, 16)

Black femmes, girls, and women bring together their material bodies and discursive selves to show how identity construction, based on their lived realities, is dynamic, flexible, and beyond prescribed boundaries. Consider the African American, Caribbean American, and African girls who participate in the program organized by Dill and others. What Dill and her co-authors show is that these girls make a whole of who they are by "embracing their Afro-Caribbean and West African identities" in a way that is not "an oppositional engagement with Blackness and an African American identity." They do so by formulating community that is in sync with their understandings of self and by "draw[ing] upon their own internal resources as they subsist and conceive of their own future identities, opportunities, and experiences" (this volume). Therein lies their magic.

Rather textually or in performance, Black femmes, girls, and women are often fragmentally presented. Making a whole out of fragments is at times improvisational, literary, spoken, or captured in images or a song, but it is always creative and generative. It is part of the process of (re)writing our understanding of the meaning of Black femmes, girls, and Black womanhood. Making a whole represents a formulation of a response to historical, current, and future renditions of Black girlhood and womanhood.

Neither Sacred nor Secular

The second theme of the book entails the authors' explorations of the ways in which Black femmes, girls, and women create a space that is not bound by an understanding of sacredness and/or secularism. David (this volume) captures one understanding of the notion that #BlackGirlMagic, and what she refers to as "affirmation codes," create a space that is neither sacred nor secular for Black girls, femmes, and women. She posits: "Fanta identifies her Afrofuturistic inspiration for her crowning glory. Her invocation of a cosmic motivation for her hair is spiritual, even as the style itself reflects a kind of technical geometry to secure it in place. Her coils also subtly signify the two rounded buns worn by Princess Leia in the *Star Wars* film franchise. Fanta's locs both seem familiar and distant at the same time" (emphasis added). When we speak of neither sacred nor secular, we are referring to that space created by Black femmes, girls, and women that blends the known, or the material, with the unknown, the spiritual and material realms, and that which cannot be easily defined to create their own sense of being. Black femmes, girls, and women create, through the labors of their magic, an alternative space and temporality.

Through their labors, Black femmes, girls, and women create a type of space that seemingly transcends boundaries. This is the type of space Royster discusses in relation to African American women writers. As argued by Royster, African American women writers engage the "ongoing task, [which] has been to create a space where no space 'naturally' existed and to raise voices that those who were entitled to speak did not welcome and were not particularly compelled to acknowledge" (2000, 233). More often than not, Black femmes, women, and girls, both writers and nonwriters (in the formal sense) alike, create this space by operating on the margins, which, according to hooks, is a source of "radical openness," in that it "affirms and sustains our subjectivity, which gives us a new location from which to articulate our sense of the world" (1990, 153). They create and enter into these spaces as a way of healing, which is a form of justice.

This is where the notion of spirituality becomes relevant for the conceptualization and use of magic among Black femmes, girls, and women. In her study on African American women's understanding and conceptualization of spirituality and religion, Jacqueline Mattis asserts, "Spirituality was variously conceptualized as one's relationship with God, with self, and/or with transcendent forces, including nature. The relationship with God or a Higher Power was associated with the experience of power, freedom, wisdom, and creativity and the transcendence of limits. . . . For these women, spirituality is the dynamic experience of both going inward and going outward" (2000, 115, 116). Dill et al., in their analysis of African American and Caribbean American adolescent girls, capture this notion of going inward and outward when they suggest that the girls are "self-reflective about their past experiences, [and] their familial and social relationships" as a means of tapping into "their own personal power amidst trials and tribulations, while being in community . . . and building sisterhood" (this volume). This, in essence, suggests how Black girls and women exist in a realm that is neither sacred nor secular. As articulated by Robinson, "Black girlhood as an organizing construct [is] invested in alternative modes of being . . . as central to building power through our relationship and accountability to one another" (this volume). The space that is neither secular nor sacred allows Black femmes, girls, and women to resist the "otherness" they often confront in their daily lives, to form community and to go within so that they can outwardly and/or otherworldly exist.

This creation of space also becomes a part of the tradition of transnational Black feminist discourse as articulated by Harrison in her chapter "Movement Makers: A Historical Analysis of Black Women's Magic in Social Movement Formation." Harrison connects #BlackGirlMagic to the grassroots Black British feminist movement of the 1970s and 1980s to show how #BlackGirlMagic is part of a lineage of Black women's self-valuation and movement-building to achieve freedom and justice. As she argues,

> A section promoting books written by Black women. This is illus-
> trated later in other print media, including *Outwrite* in which a
> "Books" section often graced the last few pages of an issue. Similarly,
> #BlackGirlMagic offers the possibility of not just documenting events
> but real-time engagement with other Black women who see themselves
> in the storyline of the hashtag. Technology not only allows one to see
> the inciting moment someone like CaShawn Thompson invented the
> phrase, but also creates an avenue through which thousands begin to
> speak back. (this volume)

The community-building aspect is key to Black girls and women existing in a space that is neither secular nor sacred. Frame, Williams, and Green (1999) suggest that there is a relationship between community and spirituality among Black women that allows them to engage in and with transgressive practices. Garner, through her exploration of SOLHOT, provides a nuanced understanding of how Black girls engage Black girlhood spirituality and, in essence, transgress. As Garner argues, "Black girlhood spirituality allows us to engage Black girlhood, and their experiences teach us how we encounter the divine in our day-to-day experiences. It allows us to see the ways that Black girlhood, in its everydayness, is sacred and holy. Black girlhood spirituality points us to the embodiment of the divine/invisible realm as being linked to our knowledge production, our bodies, and our future. Black girlhood spirituality allows us to reimagine Black girlhood as not exclusive to binaries, but inclusive of all that lies in between" (this volume). It is their creativity that affords Black femmes, girls, and women the opportunity to make community, thereby allowing them the collective power to complicate boundaries of race, gender, class, sexuality, and other vectors of identity—as defined in both the secular and sacred worlds. This brings us to the notion of speculative freedom, which is part of Black femmes', girls', and women's labor of making themselves visible.

Speculative Freedom

Black femmes, girls, and women "mobilize ideas to transform circumstances for the purpose of envisioning power differently," thereby imagining "us in the future that we, Black girls [and femmes and women] have already created" (Garner, this volume). Speculation, a critique of justice unserved, helps connect the past with the present to fulfill a future hindered but not stolen. Individually and collectively, the chapters show that BlackGirlMagic is a form of theorization that imagines and makes real the vision that Black girls and women have of themselves—this is the element of restoration. Black femmes, girls, and women, on and offline, are constructing alternative affirming personas, representations, and images that challenge dominant depictions, used primarily by the white heteronormative power structure, and are engaging in a project of cultural and (to some extent) political activism. The authors, in the words of Myisha Priest, show "just who else she [Black femmes, girls, and women] might be, what other faces she might reveal, and how that expanded vision might open up foreclosed boundaries of belonging" (2014, 461).

Black femmes, girls, and women are imagining girlhood, womanhood, and personhood differently, and, to this end, they call on memory and hauntings as a guide for a new future. They do such by providing genuine stories of Black femmes, girls, and women that in contemporary time allow them to continue "a longstanding tradition

of transnational Black feminist organizing, placing time-honored revolutionary practices within a distinctly twenty-first-century context"
(Harrison, this volume). The authors who comprise this collection
write to fill "a theoretical gap in our ability to more effectively conceptualize such agentic resistance" (Dill et al.) expressed by Black
femmes, girls, and women. As such, the authors themselves are engaging in a form of speculative freedom by creating a new set of knowledge. The authors are enacting a form of #BlackGirlMagic.

As suggested by Robinson, "SOLIIOT depends on Black women
and girls being in collective relationship to one another. This interdependence generates an articulation of power recognized as magic
that relies on building community where you live, through collective worldmaking with Black women and girls, to imagine political
power outside of capitalism" (this volume). Black girls, as argued by
Jacobs, also engage in this form of speculative freedom by deploying "Black girl critical literacies," not simply to respond to oppressive
structures but also to create particular images of themselves that are
grounded in their identities. What Jacobs suggests is that Black girls
attending independent schools "create a unique set of competences
and strategies" that include "developing critical consciousness, emotional literacy, and agency and activism" (this volume). David shows
us another means by which Black femmes and women engage in a
form of speculative freedom-vis-à-vis Afropunk. Her understanding
of "new Black femininities" offers space for "cultural citizenship" that
pushes the boundaries of the perceived prototypical Black woman.
We argue that these are the critical components necessary for Black
femmes', girls', and women's speculation and articulation of freedom.

We deploy these themes—making whole out of fragments, creating space that is neither sacred or secular, and deploying speculative freedom—to conceptualize (if we may be so bold) the four core
elements that constitute #BlackGirlMagic. What we argue is that the
three dominant themes (and you the reader may find more since there

is no one truth) show how Black femmes, girls, and women practice #BlackGirlMagic. That is, the themes show us how Black femmes, girls, and women curate and deploy their stories as a form of intra-communication methodology for community building, which then allows them to challenge dehumanizing representations, making them visible in a world that tends to render them invisible with the hope of restoring a sense of justice and freedom—their humanity. This, we argue, makes #BlackGirlMagic part of the long lineage of Black feminist cultural and political behaviors that seek to organize around the politics of identity, to challenge power in hopes of achieving justice.

Conclusion

There is a pressing question that remains: Is #BlackGirlMagic an effective strategy of dissent from the dominant and oppressive structures faced by Black femmes, girls, and women? Some read #BlackGirlMagic as inclusive, as it does not rely on a prototypical Black femme, girl, or woman. But does it address the otherness faced by Black femmes, girls, and women across time and space? If so, how? How does use of the term *magic* subvert Western thought that is grounded in positivism, rationalization, and empiricism? The various themes that link the chapters that make up this edited volume bring us a little closer to answering these questions. As a collection, the chapters show how Black femmes, girls, and women choose to "gaze back" at neoliberalism and multiple, interlocking structures of oppression.

Nevertheless, we need to think through the limitations of #BlackGirlMagic as a cultural and political response to oppression faced by Black femmes, girls, and women. Not all Black women agree with this concept. Linda Chavers, trained at New York University and Harvard, wrote in *Elle* that Black girls aren't magical, they are human (2016). Janell Hobson's analysis of Black-women-centered online projects (around the theme of beauty) led her to conclude, "A black beauty project must now grapple with a more complex examination of the intersections of race, gender, class, sexuality, and disability that can reframe black embodiment beyond commercialized spectacles and toward more diverse representations of liberated bodies" (2016). Based on this analysis, we have to critically analyze which bodies are allowed to be centered in #BlackGirlMagic and how, for example, class, sexuality, and able-bodiedness influence such. Yes, #BlackGirlMagic serves to create "space for women [femmes and girls] of color to create and survive" (Johnson and Nuñez 2015, 48). But who is allowed into that space? And who is not?

Note

1.   The UN Women (2018) report offers data on North Africa and western Asia; as a result of this grouping we decided to focus on sub-Saharan Africa.

Works Cited

Alexander-Floyd, Nikol G. 2012. "Disappearing Acts: Reclaiming Intersectionality in the Social Sciences in a Post-Black Feminist Era." *Feminist Formations* 24 (1): 1–25.

Black Demographics. n.d. "Poverty in America." http://blackdemographics .com/households/poverty/.

Bobo, Jacqueline. 1995. *Black Women as Cultural Readers*. New York: Columbia University Press.

Brown, Kimberly Juanita. 2015. *The Repeating Body: Slavery's Visual Resonance in the Contemporary*. Durham, N.C.: Duke University Press.

Brown, Ruth Nicole. 2009. *Black Girlhood Celebration: Toward a Hip-Hop Feminist Pedagogy*. New York: Peter Lang.

Brown, Ruth Nicole. 2013. *Hear Our Truths: The Creative Potential of Black Girlhood*. Urbana: University of Illinois Press.

Castells, Manuel. 2012. *Networks of Outrage and Hope: Social Movements in the Internet Age*. Malden, Mass.: Polity Press.

Chavers, Linda. 2016. *Elle*. January 13. http://www.elle.com/life-love/a33180 /why-i-dont-love-blackgirlmagic/.

Cobb, Jasmine Nichole. 2015. *Picture Freedom: Remaking Black Visuality in the Early Nineteenth Century*. New York: New York University Press.

Collins, Patricia Hill. 2000. *Black Feminist Thought: Knowledge, Consciousness, and the Politics of Empowerment*. 2nd ed. New York: Routledge.

Cooper, Anna J. 1995. "The Status of Women in America." In *Words of Fire: An Anthology of African-American Feminist Thought*, edited by B. Guy Sheftall, 44–49. New York: New Press.

Cox, Aimee M. 2015. *Shapeshifters: Black Girls and the Choreography of Citizenship*. Durham, N.C.: Duke University Press.

Crenshaw, Kimberlé. 1989. "Demarginalizing the Intersection of Race and Sex: A Black Feminist Critique of Antidiscrimination Doctrine, Feminist Theory and Antiracist Politics." *University of Chicago Legal Forum* 140: 149–67.

Crenshaw, Kimberlé Williams, Andre J. Ritchie, Rachel Anspach, Rachel Gilmer, and Luke Harris. 2015. *Say Her Name: Resisting Police Brutality against Black Women*. African American Policy Forum. New York: Center for Intersectionality and Social Policy Studies. http://static1.squarespace .com/static/53f20d90e4b0b80451158d8c/t/560c068ee4b0af26f72741df /1443628686535/AAPF_SMN_Brief_Full_singles-min.pdf.

Davis, Christina. 1988. "Interview with Toni Morrison." *Presence Africaine* 145: 141–50.

Dionne, Evette. 2013. "Black Girls Are from the Future." *Clutch*. http://clutch magonline.com/2013/03/black-girls-are-from-the-future/.

DuMonthier, Asha, Chandra Childers, and Jessica Milli. 2017. "The Status of Black Women in the United States." Institute for Policy Research. https:// iwpr.org/wp-content/uploads/2017/06/The-Status-of-Black-Women-6.26 .17.pdf.

El-Hadi, Nehal. 2015. "Radical Curation: Taking Care of Black Women's Narratives." *Model View Culture*, no. 21. https://modelviewculture.com/pieces /radical-curation-taking-care-of-black-womens-narratives.

Farmer, Paul E., Bruce Nizeye, Sara Stulac, and Salmaan Keshavjee. 2006. "Structural Violence and Clinical Medicine." *PLoS Med* 3 (10): e449. https://doi.org/10.1371/journal.pmed.0030449.

Frame, Marsha. W., Carbmen B. Williams, and Evelyn L. Green. 1999. "Balm in Gilead: Spiritual Dimensions in Counseling African American

Women." *Journal of Multicultural Counseling and Development* 27 (4): 182–92.

Garza, Alicia. 2014. "A Herstory of the #BlackLivesMatter Movement." *The Feminist Wire*. http://www.thefeministwire.com/2014/10/blacklivesmatter-2/.

Gaunt, Kyra. 2006. *The Games Black Girls Play: Learning the Ropes from Double-Dutch to Hip-Hop*. New York: New York University Press.

Graham, Erika, Craig Quinn, and Mara Brock Akil. 2015. *Being Mary Jane*. Season 2, episode 10. Directed by Rob Hardy. Performed by Gabrielle Union on April 7. Black Entertainment Television.

Hall, Stuart. 1982. "The Rediscovery of 'Ideology': Return of the Repressed in Media Studies." In *Culture, Society and the Media*, edited by Michael Gurevitch et al., 56–90. New York: Methuen.

Harris, Duchess. 2018. *Black Feminist Politics from Kennedy to Trump*. New York: Palgrave Macmillan.

Hobson, Janell. 2016. "Black Beauty and Digital Spaces." *Ada: A Journal of Gender and New Media and Technology* 10. http://adanewmedia.org/2016/10/issue10-hobson/.

hooks, bell. 1984. *Feminist Theory from Margin to Center*. Boston, Mass.: South End Press.

hooks, bell. 1990. *Yearning: Race, Gender, and Cultural Politics*. Boston, Mass.: South End Press.

Hurston, Zora Neale. 1990. *Their Eyes Were Watching God*. New York: Harper and Row.

Jarmon, Renina. n.d. "What Is *Black Girls Are from the Future*? Meaning and History." *Black Girls Are from the Future*. http://blackgirlsarefromthefuture.com/what-is-black-girls-are-from-the-future-2/.

Johnson, Jessica Marie, and Kismet Nuñez. 2015. "Alter Egos and Infinite Literacies, Part III: How to Build a Real Gyrl in 3 Easy Steps." *Black Scholar* 45 (4): 47–61.

Jordan-Zachery, Julia S. 2017. *Shadow Bodies: Black Women, Ideology, Representation, and Politics*. New Brunswick, N.J.: Rutgers University Press.

Jordan-Zachery, Julia S., and Nikol G. Alexander-Floyd. 2018. *Black Women in Politics: Demanding Justice, Challenging Power, Seeking Justice*. Albany: State University of New York Press.

Kelly, Ursula A. 1997. *Schooling Desire: Literacy, Cultural Politics, and Pedagogy*. New York: Routledge.

Mattis, Jacqueline. 2000. "African American Women's Definitions of Spirituality and Religiosity." *Journal of Black Psychology* 26 (1): 101–22.

McDonald, Soraya Nadia. 2014. "Black Twitter: A Virtual Community Ready to Hashtag out a Response to Cultural Issues." *Washington Post*. https://www.washingtonpost.com/lifestyle/style/black-twitter-a-virtual-community-ready-to-hashtag-out-a-response-to-cultural-issues/2014/01/20/41ddacf6-7ec5-11e3-9556-4a4bf7bcbd84_story.html?utm_term=.9cc341b07b5d.

McGirt, Ellen. 2017. *Fortune*. March 29. http://fortune.com/2017/03/29/black womenatwork/.

Morris, Monique W. 2016. *Pushout: The Criminalization of Black Girls in Schools*. New York: New Press.

Nash, Jennifer C. 2014. *The Black Body in Ecstasy: Reading Race, Reading Pornography*. Durham, N.C.: Duke University Press.

Priest, Myisha. 2014. "Gospels According to Faith: Rewriting Black Girlhood through the Quilt." *Children's Literature Association Quarterly* 39 (4): 461–81.

Richardson, Marilyn. 1987. *Maria W. Stewart: America's First Black Woman Political Writer*. Bloomington: Indiana University Press.

Royster, Francesca T. 2000. *Becoming Cleopatra: The Shifting Image of an Icon*. New York: Palgrave Macmillan.

Sandberg, Sheryl. 2013. *Lean In: Women, Work, and the Will to Lead*. New York: Alfred A. Knopf.

Sandoval, Chela. 2000. *Methodology of the Oppressed*. Minneapolis: University of Minnesota Press.

Sesko, Amanda K., and Monica Biernat. 2010. "Prototypes of Race and Gender: The Invisibility of Black Women." *Journal of Experimental Social Psychology* 46 (2): 356–60.

Thomas, Dexter. 2015. "Why Everyone's Saying 'Black Girls Are Magic.'" *LA Times*. September 9. http://www.latimes.com/nation/nationnow/la-na-nn-everyones-saying-black-girls-are-magic-20150909-htmlstory.html.

Thompson, CaShawn. 2013. *#BlackGirlsAreMagic*. Twitter. December 19. https://twitter.com/thepbg/status/413848553937580032.

United Nations Entity for Gender Equality and the Empowerment of Women (UN Women). 2018. "Turning Promises into Action: Gender Equality in the 2030 Agenda for Sustainable Development." http://www.unwomen.org/-/media/headquarters/attachments/sections/library/publications/2018/sdg-report-fact-sheet-latin-america-and-the-caribbean-en.pdf?la=en&vs=3555.

Walker, Alice. 1983. *In Search of Our Mothers' Gardens: Womanist Prose.* New York: Harcourt.

West, Cornel. 1989. "Black Culture and Postmodernism." In *Remaking History*, edited by Barbara Kruger and Phil Mariani, 87–96. Seattle, Wash.: Bay Press.

Williams, Jesse. 2016. Acceptance speech for the BET Awards 16. Filmed June 26, Los Angeles, Calif. Black Entertainment Television.

Wilson, J. 2003. "One Way or Another: Black Feminist Visual Theory." In *The Feminism and Visual Culture Reader*, edited by Amelia Jones, 22–25. New York: Routledge.

Woods, Jamila, vocalist. 2016. "Blk Girl Soldier." Audio. Prod. Jus Cuz x SABA. Jagjaguwar. January 19.

CHAPTER 1

MOVEMENT MAKERS

A Historical Analysis of Black Women's Magic
in Social Movement Formation

Rashida L. Harrison

Introduction

#BlackGirlMagic, a social and political phenomenon of the modern
moment, emerged on Twitter in 2012 as a collective for Black women
and girls to celebrate who they are; it gained traction by arming them
with the full use of the technological tools of their time (Sinclair 2016).
#BlackGirlMagic is part of an emerging sphere of social experiences
where thoughts and ideas, communicated via a hashtag, act as a cat-
alyst for building community. Black women, however, are not new to
such culturally centered efforts to build and sustain community. For
example, a search of the hashtag unleashes historical tropes and tools
critical to Black British feminist organizing in the 1970s and 1980s,
including affective political engagement and a quest to belong and
be part of a community that understands how to exist when power
and capital are not readily disposable, as well as the pursuit to secure
economic resources that amount to social and political power. In fact,
#BlackGirlMagic offers a modern-day construction of transnational
Black feminist praxis. Several Black feminist scholars contribute to
the genealogy of the term *transnational Black feminism* and offer similar, yet complex, descriptions (Boyce Davies 2008; Fisher 2012). For
the purposes of this chapter, transnational Black feminist praxis refers

to the intersectional political, economic, social, and cultural work done by Black-identified women across national borders to facilitate women's liberation. Social media creates unique opportunities for Black women to bypass traditional power structures, to develop ideas and movements that reflect the realities of their lives, and to enable those ideas to generate interest and catalyze the establishment of virtual communities that transcend nation-state borders.

In this chapter, I situate the work of Black British feminists, organizing in the 1970s and 1980s, in a tradition of transnational Black feminist praxis operationalized within a framework of #BlackGirlMagic. I illustrate that such #BlackGirlMagic facilitates Black women's cultural bridge building, endeavors toward economic mobility, and the creation of political platforms—all important ingredients to the politics of solidarity. I do this first by offering #BlackGirlMagic as a theoretical frame consistent with larger frameworks of transnational Black feminist praxis. Although BlackGirlMagic has existed for as long as there have been Black girls—which is to say, since the dawn of humanity—I emphasize the advent of the hashtag #BlackGirlMagic, noting the way it resonates with a broad audience of Black-identified women. Next, I interrogate the potential of social media and the hashtag as a tool for mobilizing and disseminating information about broader global social movements. Third, I draw on historical collections of newspapers and pamphlets from UK-based Black feminist organizations of the 1970s and 1980s to interrogate how Black women historically worked across national borders to build solidarity, community, and political movements. I draw on the Organisation of Women of African and Asian Decent (OWAAD) and *Outwrite* newspaper to highlight the distinctive transnational rhetoric of the Black British feminist movement, as providing longstanding models for global Black feminist organizing strategies. Finally, I illustrate that the cultural bridge building by way of a hashtag is an organic means of deploying a politics of solidarity critical to the transnational Black feminist networks and praxis of those networks of the past. In the contemporary moment, #BlackGirlMagic is a critical tool for building transnational Black feminist social movements, and ultimately #BlackGirlMagic reinforces a tradition of community building that creates spaces of belonging for Black women.

Framing #BlackGirlMagic

#BlackGirlMagic, in its everyday use, celebrates the "universal everyday awesomeness of black women" (Wilson 2016). It is about acknowledging the cultural, social, political, and economic advancements of Black women, and is poised to provide inspiration via the trending hashtag. It began with CaShawn Thompson, a layperson working as a caregiver in Washington, D.C., who used Twitter to express "Black Girls are Magic" (quoted in Thomas 2015). In doing so, she unwittingly named the long-simmering movement and set the stage for it to penetrate all corners of the globe. The hashtag refers to the celebration of Black women's everyday accomplishments, including achievements that are inspirational and extraordinary given the socioeconomic and political challenges facing Black women as marginalized citizens across the globe. The idea appeals to millions of people, many who are indeed politically Black women of varying ethnic and even racial identities (Swaby 2014). It effectively acts as a rallying call for a new era of Black women's work that spans a variety of cultural, political, and economic spaces.

#BlackGirlMagic has become a tool for social-movement building in the tradition of transnational Black feminist discourse. As a concept, transnational Black feminism assumes an interconnection of social phenomena across geospatial locales. Social phenomena such as the problematic constructions of race, class, gender, sexuality, ethnicity, and religion are, in many ways, connected to notions of geography, identity, history, and home. In an era where a hashtag operates and generates such connections, #BlackGirlMagic may also facilitate the bridge for the connection of such identities, fostering a politics of solidarity—an important, yet often contested, social capital of activist feminists (Collins 2014; Sinclair 2016). Transnational Black feminism, as an organizing practice, often challenges and redefines what it means to be Black and a woman in oppressive spaces; by challenging existing notions of Blackness and womanhood particularly within Western capitalist systems, Black women discover the power to define that which more accurately reflects the realities of their lives.

The Magic of [Social] Media and Social Movements

While #BlackGirlMagic is a recent phenomenon, and it has some new tools at its disposal thanks to technological advancements, the principles guiding it as praxis are but the latest incarnation of transnational Black women's resistance movements. Transnational movements, like larger social movements, begin with interest and recognition (Tarrow 2011, 11). As they emerge, these movements may assume varying modalities, so long as participants recognize, affirm, and organize around shared interests and principles. The rise of social media ushers in a new era of worldwide social and political interaction. Platforms like Facebook, Twitter, and YouTube connect rank-and-file citizens with similar perspectives and political critiques. Admittedly, "the use of social media tools—text messaging, email, photo sharing, social networking, and the like—does not have a single pre-ordained outcome" (Shirky 2011, 29); however, the basic ability for citizens of different nation states to interact with newfound velocity and efficiency makes social media a primary factor of analysis for any twenty-first-century social movement.

Like the women who consciously worked to create transnational activist networks during Black feminist movements of the 1970s and

1980s, the women driving #BlackGirlMagic are motivated by a shared desire to reconfigure unequal social structures, achieve sociopolitical recognition, and gain respect and unfettered access to the societal benefits of full citizenship. There is a long tradition of revolutionary organizing theory undergirding the development of political collectives. This activism—an important byproduct of enhanced social interaction and burgeoning cultural literacy—reflects the historical experiences of marginalized populations. In decades past, when modes of communication were more easily controlled by repressive nation states, marginalized peoples were often forced to travel to the epicenter of global empires to access elusive economic opportunities. Nevertheless, the increased access to technology by historically disenfranchised groups creates the conditions for critical media literacies (McArthur 2016). Such literacies have the potential to replicate the media forces generated for political education by Black movements of the past.

Despite institutional forces, Black Power, for example, which coalesced into a movement, spread through cultural expression such as music and art and print media, including journalistic endeavors and newspaper creation (Jennings 2015). Boyce Davies (2008) emphasizes the role of journalism in the political life of Claudia Jones, an example that offers a case study in the historical evolution of a transnational Black feminist. Jones founded and managed London's first major Black newspaper, the *West Indian Gazette and Afro-Asian Caribbean News* (Schwarz 2003, 268). Newspapers, for diaspora communities, are an instrumental source of information, especially when the dispersal is made up of communities of the politically exiled. Such dissemination, however, was, and continues to be, limited by normal human processes, including the existence of nation-state borders. Nevertheless, the journalistic endeavors of activists working across borders, including those of Black British feminists, is part of the history of migration of Black citizens and immigrants alike. Often, these individuals relocated to major Western and First World nations in order to provide for the families left behind in their native satellite countries; they would abide in transient spaces, maintain dual citizenship, and remain active in a home country's political and economic arena (Tarrow 2005, 2–3). The condition of cultural interconnectedness and mobility across space, which defined their existence, no longer requires international migration or the formation of cross-cultural identities—it can be achieved via ownership of a smartphone, Internet access, and a social media account. By leveraging these new technologies, an *ordinary* citizen like Thompson can build political currency around a public affirmation, pioneer a global economic brand, and incite a global community of women.

Social movements that cross nation-state borders are historically important for people connected by histories of colonization, and to this day they remain vital to the survival of critical cultural identities. Contemporary movements constructed to preserve cultural values via strategic resistance are growing more quickly than ever before and, in the process, are setting new standards for modern social movement building. The world watched the social media-fueled rise of the Arab Spring, which set a new template for the ways in which movements are birthed, actualized, and witnessed by an increasingly international public (NPR 2011). By crowdsourcing frustrated voices, progressive principles, and strategies of resistance among the disenfranchised in Tunisia, Egypt, Libya, and Yemen, social media helped shape a revolutionary fervor that continues to threaten traditional power structures in that part of the world (*NPR* 2011). In the United States, these new technologies fuel the popular rise of nontraditional progressive politicians like President Barack Obama and Bernie Sanders (Auerbach and Brogan 2016). And, most closely related to #BlackGirlMagic is the new global Black Lives Matter movement, which began as a hashtag tweeted in response to the acquittal of George Zimmerman in the murder of a young Black adolescent, Trayvon Martin (Kamp 2016).

Black women participating in #BlackGirlMagic also facilitate the global coalescing of Black communities. Like organized movements of the past, and more specifically that of the Black British feminist movement, many modern Black movement makers view "Black" as a multilayered descriptor of racial and political identity, formed from a variety of cultural, linguistic, religious, and political affiliations; it is both performativity and dialogic (Swaby 2014, 13). More largely, transnational Black feminist praxis recognizes personal identities as multidimensional, and contextualizes identity construction as a social process that is fluid rather than fixed; Black women form personal and political identities in myriad ways, and those identities may shift depending on the social, political, and economic realities of their time. Finally, a critical organizing principle borrowed from historical Black women's movements is the adoption of a politic of solidarity among women fighting oppression globally. Women recognize that their oppression is not isolated from feminists' struggles in other nations, and commit to unifying their efforts as a means to advance common goals and more effectively oppose a shared enemy. By utilizing these shared principles of resistance, particularly in the realm of the cyber world, #BlackGirlMagic unifies seemingly disparate global feminist political agendas under the "Black" banner, and constructs a formidable force of activists to combat systemic repression of women in all corners of the world. An examination of the history of such a political practice is important for establishing a global precedent of Black women's organizing across national and state boundaries.

The Case of the Black British Feminist Movement

The Black British feminist movement evolved in a political moment where *politically Black*–identified women sought to politically, economically, and socially belong in a country where the imperial power structures actively opposed them (Swaby 2014; Mirza 1997; Rassool 1997). The movement began with organization building, including the launch of the Brixton Black Women's Group in 1973, the Manchester inauguration of the Black Women's Cooperative in 1975, the creation of OWAAD in 1978, and later continued to thrive with the founding of writing collectives such as *Outwrite*, which produced its first publication in 1982. These, and other, organizations recognized that to be Black and British meant multiethnic, immigrant, and contested citizenship. Therefore, the reach of their political concerns was often connected to, and inclusive of, homelands outside of Great Britain's geographic boundaries.

The racialization of immigrants to England emerged with an influx of South Asians, African, and Caribbean Black and brown people in the post–World War II era because of the long history of British Empire building. Inhabitants of countries within the British Empire were led to believe they enjoyed full British citizenship and were entitled to all of the associated benefits (Paul 1997, 10–13). Nevertheless, when Black and brown soldiers, nurses, and workers from countries including Jamaica, Trinidad, India, Pakistan, Sri Lanka, Nigeria, and Ghana sought to take advantage of the promises of "the mother country," they were met with backlash. In the late 1960s, a massive anti-immigrant and anti-Black campaign erupted in England alongside a series of nationality and immigration legislative acts creating separate and unequal tiers of membership in the country (Perry 2015). The history of mass immigration, as well as the racist rhetoric that undergirded the momentum to minimize British Empire citizens from full participation in society, is one that is recently documented within the last twenty years (Perry 2015, 10). Black British women, however, challenged this notion as early as the 1970s using the language of racism and imperialism to capture the experience they faced in their country as well as within the British women's liberation movement.

Black British feminist organizing developed in a political context that conceived of people who are nonwhite and immigrant as an inherent threat to the imperial narrative of British life (Paul 1997,

9–14). The evolving identity politics in the late 1970s is evident in the formation of organizations such as OWAAD and later *Outwrite*; although ethnic, religious, and class differences were central in the organization, the lack of attention to the salience of those differences ultimately threatened the potential for Black multiethnic coalition building (Fisher 2012, 84; Mirza 1997, 8–9). The acknowledgment of shared politics occurred in the form of short pamphlets and zines, with the earliest published texts occurring in 1985, and later scholarly inquiring in 1997 (Mirza 1997). *The Heart of the Race* (1985), one of the first Black British feminists' texts, focused specifically on Afro-Caribbean people. The authors, Beverley Bryan, Stella Dadzie, and Suzanne Scafe, endeavored to explain how their activist lives, up until that point, were limited to Black men struggling for racial equality and white women working inside of the women's liberation movement. The authors reflect a political tradition similar to the U.S.-based Combahee River Collective when they write,

> That our race, our class, and our sex have combined to determine the quality of our lives, both in the Caribbean and in Britain, is undisputed. . . . But what matters to us is the *way* Black women have challenged this triple state of bondage. . . . If we are to gain anything from our history and form our lives in this country . . . we must take stock of our experiences, assess our responses—and learn from them. Our aim has been to tell it as *we* know it placing our story within its history at the heart of our race. (Bryan, Dadzie, and Scafe 1985, 2)

The focus on Caribbean Black women was critical to framing politically Black, but ethnically diverse, experiences of women in England. It made clear that those women who identified as Black were former, and sometimes current, inhabitants of British colonies. The text is a product of some central questions grappling with the culpability of solidarity politics in the presence of difference. It is an early precedent to ongoing conversations, even today, about *whose* Blackness is politicized (Nassool 1997; Swaby 2014). This trend of solidarity through difference is not often a conscious politic. "Sameness, difference and complexity are built into an understanding of Black British Feminism" (Anim-Ado 2014, 57).

OWAAD, launched in February of 1978 by fifteen Black women of varying ethnic African, Asian, and Caribbean identities, was created as an umbrella organization for the range of grassroots Black women's groups emerging during the period (Fisher 2012; Brixton Black Women's Group 1984). In the draft of OWAAD's constitution was the assertion that they rejected "all unnecessary distinctions between these two groups of Black people" (OWAAD 1980). They affirmed that women (of color) in Britain are victims of a colonial history that leaves them in the same class in society where racism and economics are exploitative factors. OWAAD's framework of conscious intentions toward reconstructing social status while fashioning a shared politically Black identity (Swaby 2014) informs the ways in which Black women operate in the era of technological connectivity in the United Kingdom specifically, and abroad more generally.

OWAAD fostered connectivity in important ways by publishing a monthly newsletter entitled *FOWAAD!* and by holding forums and conferences (Brixton Black Women's Group 1984, 84). In 1980, OWAAD produced a special pamphlet that was a result of a collection of talks given at the National Black Women's Conference in Brixton, London, in March 1979. The conference was organized to bring together "Asian Indo-and Afro-Caribbean and African Sisters and Black Sisters born and brought up here [Britain]" (OWAAD 1980, 1). This pamphlet, entitled *Black Women in Britain Speak Out* (OWAAD 1980), outlined specific social, political, and economic concerns of Black women. There were write-ups that tackled identity politics and explained how they defined Blackness. There was also a

pointed discussion about how the U.S.-initiated Black Power movement influenced the organization. The authors wrote,

> Black people reassert their identity and self-esteem, rejecting the neg-
> ative labels and roles which we have been forced to accept in the past.
> For our purposes, we will use the term "black" to refer to the two major
> ethnic groups of black people in this country. Those people who came
> originally from the Indian Subcontinent, many via East Africa or the
> Caribbean, and those people who have their origins in Africa, or who
> as a result of slavery now have their immediate origins in a number of
> Caribbean countries. (OWAAD 1980, 1A)

While acknowledging differences, OWAAD took the position that,
despite cultural and ethnic differences between the groups, they did
not distinguish unless necessary to "refer *specifically*" (1980, 1A). The
groups involved had joint historical experiences with colonialism,
and more critical is their common "second class citizen status" in a
racist society, which implored them to have a firm bond. "Our Unity
arises from a common experience of an oppression which is historical, racial, sexist and economic. . . . Our use of the single term Black
is one way of stressing this unity" (1980, 1A).

On March 8, 1982, International Women's Day, the first issue of
Outwrite was distributed throughout Britain. *Outwrite* had an inter-
nationalist stance and was committed to multiracial coalition work
("International Women's Day" 1986, 46:9A). Additionally, the newspaper professed an anti-imperialist, antiracist, framework. They wrote
articles that attended to issues of marginalized women, which, in large
part according to the editors, are "black and Third world" ("Here We
Are" 1982, 2A). The writing collective, much like its predecessors
and affiliate groups of Black women activists, worked in an interstitial structure. That is, their organization at the grassroots level often

occurred in "the cracks," where workers often volunteered and served as full-time, unpaid staff for their organizations (Springer 2001, 156).

The major themes of *Outwrite* emerge within the first several issues. In an article entitled "What the Papers Are Saying," the editors discussed the need for a women's newspaper explicitly; they wrote, "The popular press would have us in a trap . . . to play on fears and insecurities. . . . The papers make full use of sexism, racism and political ignorance; they rarely challenge them" ("What the Papers Are Saying" 1982, 1). The reference to what went on within the country is clear, but even more critical for *Outwrite* was the British occupation of areas around the world, which its citizens had little-to-no knowledge of unless it was a "crisis point." The women participating in the project articulated a strong connection with women abroad and oftentimes with what they called home: "We need to bring more news and stories from abroad or back home and regularly; news that is important to us; news that we can share in, news that we can act upon" ("Here We Are," 1982, 2A).

Similar to the activist environment facilitated by social media, there emerged overlapping textual communities that included activist women from OWAAD, *and* later, the Women, Immigration and Nationality Group, or WING, in 1985; this was in addition to more longstanding groups such as the Brixton Black Women's Group; Zimbabwe African National Union-Patriotic Front Women's League (ZANU PF); and Awaaz, an Asian women's group, to name a few (Brixton Black Women's Group 1984, 84). In various moments, many of the same women contributed articles to *Outwrite*, whether they wrote them or deployed them from more local sources in countries abroad. Women, who contributed to *Outwrite* in these communities, did so by writing in pamphlets, newspapers, or manuscripts; they often attended meetings from smaller women's groups and were active with the parents' association and Black education movement. More largely, these women worked to educate and advocate for a larger community on issues of immigration and nationality laws that impacted all of them;

they were brought together by shared political interests and concern (*Outwrite* 1982–88). Many of them would report on stories from back home, sometimes based on their own experiences traveling, and others from family, activist friends, or official reports from activist organizations they maintained contact with in other countries. Evidence of working together across groups is in *Outwrite*, where different organizations used it as an advertising platform—there was also documentation of meetings and get-togethers. Their writings illustrate intentional community building that showed solidarity while simultaneously honoring ethnic, religious, and social differences. They engaged critical questions such as, What are the conditions under which Black women organize? and, What are the limits of solidarity? Such questions were important given historical experiences and the continuous fight for a larger struggle to belong in British society. Such questions still exist today and can be facilitated by #BlackGirlMagic with an intent of creating distinctive cultural organizing tools that foster political spaces where Black women belong and have a continued impact within the global communities they construct.

OWAAD and *Outwrite*'s existence is important, having emerged during a distinct period that challenged and redefined the parameters of Black womanhood in Britain and globally. The women organizing and documenting in these groups were also in communication and solidarity with Black women in the United States, South Africa, and Egypt, as evidenced by the various articles found in the periodical during its six-year tenure (*Outwrite* 1982–88). Such praxis is integral to transnational Black feminist consciousness. The contemporary moment and organizing sphere of #BlackGirlMagic illustrates how Black women, often organically, build coalitions based on a collective understanding of larger structural forces. Those structural forces are often white supremacist and patriarchal, and constantly seek to define who they are as well as limit Black women's political agency. Additionally, in the contemporary moment, politically Black

identified women continue to grapple with the work of identity politics. #BlackGirlMagic coalesces around shared experiences of being
a Black girl or woman. Western Black feminist movements are largely
shaped by questions around differences in class, sexuality, geography, ethnicity, and religion (Abod and Lorde 2007). Since #Black-
GirlMagic moves in a space that is inherently designed to foster solidarity through difference, it has the potential for a sustained social
movement.

From Hashtag to Social Movement

The histories of Black British feminist collectives offer a frame in
which to view #BlackGirlMagic as a movement with conscious intentions to improve social, political, and economic conditions of Black
women. Much like how Black British women of the 1970s and 1980s
made connections with each other and women across national borders, #BlackGirlMagic invites Black-identified women globally to be
part of cultural, social, political, and economic assertions of their lived
experiences. Such a sentiment is communicated in the first issue of
FOWAAD!, where the editors indicate that they "hope to provide sisters everywhere with a space where you can air your views, pass on
information, and call on other sisters for support in your everyday
struggles" (OWAAD 1979). They go on to indicate the types of information they provide, including featuring poetry and art from women
of their communities, as well as a section promoting books written by
Black women. This is illustrated later in other print media, including
Outwrite in which a "Books" section often graced the last few pages
of an issue. Similarly, #BlackGirlMagic offers the possibility of not
just documenting events but real-time engagement with other Black
women who see themselves in the storyline of the hashtag. Technology not only allows one to see the inciting moment someone like
CaShawn Thompson invented the phrase, but also creates an avenue

through which thousands begin to speak back; thus, researchers can document the development of the social action incited from an idea that Black girls are magic.

#BlackGirlMagic fosters virtual collectives, much like groups or political organizations of the past, acting as a launching point for both for-profit and nonprofit ventures headed by Black women. It serves as a key platform for educating the broader society about the ways in which power infiltrates every aspect of society. #BlackGirlMagic is apparent from the official political realm where figures like former First Lady Michelle Obama worked to establish policies that critically address the health and development of Black girls and women—to the fashion and entertainment world where Black women continue to revolutionize worldwide standards of beauty and exceptionality. The seemingly ordinary aspects of Black women's lives have become sources of magic transported across the globe via hashtag.

#BlackGirlMagic's bridge building in the sphere of social media can have important social and economic capital gains. The results of its circulation in cyberspace include the creation of a T-shirt line by credited handler Thompson; the launching of a number of websites with variations on the sentiment of "Black Girls are Magic," dedicated to social and political literacy around Black women's writings; and many political and social commentaries that educate larger communities about the variety of social injustices that Black women are subjected to, as well as how they work on an everyday basis to fight (Hohn 2017; *Essence* 2017). #BlackGirlMagic also operates in a complicated place where social gains may create and maintain economic inequality. Women operating at the grassroots level in the 1980s raised similar issues. An example includes the eventual demise of *Outwrite* as a publication because the collective did not have enough resources to sustain it. Those resources were about power and capital. We see similar conversations emerging, particularly when there are disagreements about who first used the hashtag or products of authenticity. Ultimately it matters because to be recognized on social media will amount to increased economic and social capital. It was only in March 2017 that Thompson launched "Black Girls are Magic" mugs, and even more recently, in June 2017, she publicly commented on the fact that she "low-balled" herself by charging under twenty dollars for shirts. She then went on to comment, "I just wanted everybody who wanted one to have access to it" (Thompson 2017). Her public discussion of both recognizing capitalistic competition but a desire to share and make accessible the positive outcomes of BlackGirl-Magic are the current dilemmas of earlier movements where women grappled with some being privileged and having different accessibility levels within a social movement (Brixton Black Women's Group 1984, 88).

Black British feminist organizing of the 1970s and 1980s is a precedent to the modern-day construction of a transnational Black feminist praxis, #BlackGirlMagic. The hashtag facilitates historical tropes of emotionally driven political engagement, a constant strife to belong and be part of a community that understands how to exist when power and capital are not readily available, as well as the quest to secure economic resources that amount to social and political power. #BlackGirlMagic is not merely about the nuanced ways in which grassroots is recreated, but rather a continuation of the forty-plus years of Black women creating social networks despite the imposition of nation-state borders. That creation of a social network is very much connected to and builds because of the politics of Blackness and Black women's praxis of building bridges. It is in the bridge of differences— national, ethnic, religious, and even racial—that Black women create and recreate solidarity politics necessary for a longstanding movement for Black women's liberation.

Works Cited

Abod, Jennifer, and Audre Lorde. 2007. *The Edge of Each Other's Battles: The Vision of Audre Lorde*. New York: Women Make Movies.

Anim-Addo, Joan. 2014. "Activist Mothers Maybe, Sisters Surely? Black British Feminism, Absence and Transformation." *Feminist Review* 108: 44–60.

Auerbach, David, and Jacob Brogan. 2016. "The Bernie Bubble." *Slate*. February 17. http://www.slate.com/articles/technology/future_tense/2016/02/the_bernie_sanders_campaign_owes_a_lot_to_social_media.html.

Boyce Davies, Carol. 2008. *Left of Karl Marx: The Political Life of Black Communist Claudia Jones*. Durham: Duke University Press.

Brixton Black Women's Group. 1984. "Black Women Organizing." *Feminist Review*, 17: 84–89.

Bryan, Beverley, Stella Dadzie, and Suzanne Scafe. 1985. *The Heart of the Race: Black Women's Lives in Britain*. London: Virago.

Collins, Christopher. 2014. "Hashtags Are the New Way to Make Money." *LinkedIn* (blog). August 8. https://www.linkedin.com/pulse/20140808094545-101772914-hashtags-are-the-new-way-to-make-money/.

Essence. 2017. "Black Girl Magic." *Essence*. http://www.essence.com/blackgirlmagic.

Fisher, Tracy. 2012. *What's Left of Blackness? Feminisms, Transracial Solidarities, and the Politics of Belonging in Britain*. New York: Palgrave Macmillan.

Hohn, Nadia L. 2017. "Black Girl Magic: Black Girlhood, Imaginations, and Activism | We Need Diverse Books." *We Need Diverse Books*. http://weneeddiversebooks.org/black-girl-magic-black-girlhood-imaginations-and-activism/.

Jarmon, Renina. 2011. "Arielle Loren Asks 'Is Beyoncé the Face of Contemporary Feminism?' My Response." *New Model Minority*. May 25. http://newmodelminority.com/2011/05/25/arielle-loren-asks-is-beyonce-the-face-of-contemporary-feminism-my-response/.

Jennings, Billy X. 2015. "Remembering the Black Panther Party Newspaper, April 25, 1967–September 1980." *San Francisco Bay View*. May 4. http://sfbayview.com/2015/05/remembering-the-black-panther-party-newspaper-april-25-1967-september-1980/.

Kamp, Karin. 2016. "Co-Founder Alicia Garza on the Black Lives Matter Movement." *BillMoyers.com*. October 3. http://billmoyers.com/story/black-lives-matter/.

McArthur, Sherell A. 2016. "Black Girls and Critical Media Literacy for Social Activism." *English Education* 48 (4): 362–79.

Mirza, Heidi Safia, ed. 1997. *Black British Feminism: A Reader*. New York: Routledge.

NPR. 2017. "The Arab Spring: A Year of Revolution." *NPR.org*. http://www.npr
.org/2011/12/17/143897126/the-arab-spring-a-year-of-revolution.

OWAAD (Organisation of Women of African and Asian Descent). 1979.
FOWAAD! July 1. London: Organisation of Women of African and Asian
Descent

OWAAD (Organisation of Women of African and Asian Descent). 1980.
Black Women in Britain Speak Out. London: Organisation of Women of
African and Asian Descent.

Outwrite. 1982–88 "Outwrite (Newspaper, 1982–1988)." Grassroots Feminism. http://www.grassrootsfeminism.net/cms/node/164/.

Outwrite. 1982a. "Here We Are." *Outwrite*. March.

Outwrite. 1982b. "What the Papers Are Saying." *Outwrite*. March.

Outwrite. 1986. "International Women's Day 1986, Diary of Events." *Outwrite*.
March.

Paul, Kathleen. 1997. *Whitewashing Britain: Race and Citizenship in the Post-
war Era*. Ithaca, N.Y.: Cornell University Press.

Perry, Kennetta Hammond. 2015. *London Is the Place for Me: Black Britons,
Citizenship, and the Politics of Race*. New York: Oxford University Press.

Rassool, Naz. 1997. "Fractured or Flexible Identities." In *Black British
Feminism: A Reader*, edited by Heidi Safia Mirza, 187–204. New York:
Routledge.

Schwarz, Bill. 2003. "'Claudia Jones and the West Indian Gazette': Reflections
on the Emergence of Post-colonial Britain." *Twentieth Century British History* 14 (3): 264–85.

Shirky, Clay. 2011. "The Political Power of Social Media." *Foreign Affairs* 90
(1): 28–41.

Sinclair, Leah. 2016. "Why We Need Movements like #BlackGirlMagic." *Dazed*.
February 18. http://www.dazeddigital.com/artsandculture/article/29854/1
/why-we-need-movements-like-blackgirlmagic.

Springer, Kimberly. 2001. "The Interstitial Politics of Black Feminist Organizations." *Meridians* 1 (2): 155–91.

Swaby, Nydia. 2014. "'Disparate in Voice, Sympathetic in Direction': Gendered
Political Blackness and the Politics of Solidarity." *Feminist Review* 108: 11–25.

Tarrow, Sidney G. 2005. *The New Transnational Activism*. New York: Cambridge University Press.

Tarrow, Sidney G. 2011. *Power in Movement: Social Movements and Conten-
tious Politics*. 3rd ed. New York: Cambridge University Press.

Thomas, Dexter. 2015. "Why Everyone's Saying 'Black Girls Are Magic.'" *LA Times*. September 9. http://www.latimes.com/nation/nationnow/la-na-nn -everyones-saying-black-girls-are-magic-20150909-htmlstory.html.

Thompson, CaShawn. 2017. "I just wanted everybody . . ." Twitter post. June 15. https://twitter.com/thepbg/status/875420970483421184.

Wilson, Julee. 2016. "The Meaning Of #BlackGirlMagic, And How You Can Get Some of It." *Huffington Post*. January 12. http://www.huffingtonpost .com/entry/what-is-black-girl-magicvideo_us_5694dad4e4b086bc1cd517f4.

CHAPTER 2

"I CAN ONLY DO ME"

African American, Caribbean American, and West African Girls' Transnational Nature of Self-Articulation

LeConté J. Dill with Shavaun S. Sutton,
Bianca Rivera, and Abena Amory-Powell

Introduction

"I told you that girl was rough around the edges," a school administrator said to me (LeConté) as I was telling Princess,[1] a seventeen-year-old high school junior, good-bye at the conclusion of our workshop. After getting to know Princess for three years, I would not describe her as "rough." When I asked Princess to describe herself, she offered "nice," "funny," and "talented." Princess beamed. "I'm just too amazing!" Black girls are often constrained within a false dichotomy of either being invisible when it comes to any intervention because of the shallow perception that they are doing just fine, or they become hypervisible and susceptible to punitive policies when they are mislabeled as the "angry Black woman." This chapter seeks to deconstruct and then complicate the narratives of Black girls and Black girlhood, as informed Black girls themselves. We detail our engagement of ethnography and participatory narrative analysis with a group of African American, Caribbean American, and West African high school and college-aged young women from Brooklyn, New York, who self-identify as Black. These girls use various strategies to navigate, negotiate, and articulate their relationships, their appearance, their behaviors, and their identities.

A Seat at the Table for Brooklyn Girls: Sitting Within Black Feminisms

The girls in our study are part of a violence intervention program in central Brooklyn. They are recruited into the program by school officials who see them as "at risk"—they cut class, they are doing poorly in school, they fight, and/or they are self-harming. Too often, society mislabels and misrecognizes these same girls as just being too much— too "loud," "angry," "deviant," and "defiant" (Koonce 2012; Morris 2007). Some youth advocates urge for a reconsideration of these girls as "in-risk" instead of "at-risk," as many of them have already experienced and currently still experience homelessness, running away from home, exposure to domestic violence, foster care, abuse and neglect, and/or teen pregnancy or parenting (Developmental Services Group 2013). By spending regular time with these young women, we as co-authors witness that their daily praxis is actually that of resistance in the very places and spaces that threaten to oppress, harm, or erase them. Since violence intervention programs are often situated in the disciplinary frameworks of medicine and public health and are placed in physical sites such as hospitals and schools, we recognize a theoretical gap in our ability to more effectively conceptualize such agentic resistance among these girls. Therefore, we look to Black feminist thought as an epistemological foundation that more accurately recognizes these girls, their experiences, and their praxes.

Black feminism brings the distinct and nuanced voices of Black women into the forefront (Bambara 1970). Black feminist thought's core themes are: (1) acknowledging a legacy of struggle by Black women; (2) attention to the interlocking nature of race, gender, and class oppression; (3) the replacement of the "controlling images" of the "asexual mammy," "promiscuous jezebel," and "emasculating sapphire," and more recent labels, such as the "gold digger," the "welfare queen," and the "baby mama," with self-defined images created for and by Black women; (4) a belief in Black women's activism as mothers, teachers, and community leaders; and (5) sensitivity to sexual politics (Collins 1990; Combahee River Collective 1977; Crenshaw 1991; Stephens and Phillips 2003; Stewart and Richardson 1987). These themes offer us an expanded frame for the work that we do with and on behalf of Black women.

In 1971, Joyce Ladner wrote that "the total misrepresentation of the Black community and the various myths which surround it can be seen in microcosm in the Black female adolescent." Her seminal work and the aforementioned foremothers of Black feminist thought inform the emergence of Black girlhood studies (Brown 2013; Cox 2015; Gaunt 2006; Jones 2009; LaBennett 2011; Love 2012; Winn 2011) in ways that are culturally sustaining and strengths-focused (Lindsay-Dennis 2015). Black girlhood studies recognize girlhood, youth, and adolescence as important developmental stages for Black girls, though these developmental stages are often invisible, constrained, or hypervisible by society. Black girlhood studies offer an understanding of Black girls' lives in more useful, nuanced, and accountable ways (Brown 2013).

Black girlhood studies scholars examine how Black girls resist the very institutions, practices, policies, and ideologies that foster their marginalization. Ruth Nicole Brown (2007) has noted that Black girls who are considered "at-risk" are targeted by social programs designed to "empower" them. Brown continues to assert that these girls have actually come to programs already having knowledge about the ways that power impacts their lives and their environments—they are conscious and #woke to the ways the media, policymakers, educators, and researchers frame them, through their own lived experiences of navigating and negotiating such spaces and systems. Aimee Meredith Cox (2015) illuminates Black girls' "shapeshifting" in order to resist their implied or circumscribed dehumanization. Oneka LaBennett's (2011) important ethnographic work with West Indian American girls in central Brooklyn highlights how they create transnational identities, particularly through their use, commodification, negotiation, and reuse of music, food, and fashion from the United States and the West Indies. Our study is also situated in central Brooklyn. The East Flatbush neighborhood where our participants go to school and where many of them live has historical and contemporary patterns of Caribbean immigration and "Caribbeanization" (LaBennett 2011). Overall, we expand the work of our #squad of Black girlhood studies scholars to examine how Black girls combine their sociopolitical "herstories" as Brooklyn girls with their current treatment, behaviors, and practices, and how they conceptualize their own futures to create an explicit praxis of Black girlhood health and wellness.

Methods

Our study is focused on a youth violence prevention program—the Kings Against Violence Initiative (KAVI)—based in a high school complex in central Brooklyn. The authors have chosen not to use a pseudonym for our research partner (KAVI). Some scholars agree that removing identifying information erases context that is valuable to research (Thomson et al. 2005). To not anonymize the research site recognizes that KAVI sits within specific historical, contemporary, geographical, and symbolic moments and meanings (Elwood and Martin 2000; Nespor 2000). KAVI's Women's Program engaged approximately forty high school–aged African American, Caribbean American, African, and Latina young women from 2011 to 2016. The 2015–16 cohort of KAVI Women's Program participants, when our ethnographic interviews took place, was approximately eighteen girls. Since the fall of 2016, participation in the KAVI Women's Program has increased to serving nearly sixty girls a year. This is due in part to organizational vision and increased staff capacity, funding, and school and community partnerships.

We use multiple and innovative methodological approaches (Few, Stephens, and Rouse-Arnett 2003; Lindsay-Dennis 2015) in order to more effectively inform our analyses of the intersections of race, gender, socioeconomic status, age, and geography about the daily experiences of urban Black girls. Qualitative and critical participatory action research methods place Black girls at the center of inquiry and analysis. I conceived of and continued to evolve this study informed by my own standpoint as a Black woman from a distressed and stigmatized neighborhood similar to East Flatbush, who is a former full-time youth development professional, a scholar-activist, a poet, and a volunteer with KAVI since 2013. In particular, all of the co-authors are African American, West Indian, and Latinx women who spent three years conducting direct and participant observation (Emerson, Fretz, and Shaw 2011) at weekly KAVI sessions. As an ethic of participatory witnessing (Banks-Wallace 2000; Lindsay-Dennis 2015), the co-authors have been sharing our own lived experiences as scholars, public health practitioners, daughters, and sisters with the participants since 2013. After gaining approval from the Institutional Review Board of the State University of New York Downstate Medical Center, we have augmented these observations with archival research of central Brooklyn and systematic social observations (Sampson and Raudenbush 1999) in the school and in the participants' home neighborhoods. Such ethnographic approaches are useful in helping us to better understand the role that environments play in reproducing or resisting multiple social forces in the lives of individuals (Burton 1997).

From a Black feminist stance, we center urban Black girls as knowledge producers for our study. Therefore, we conducted one-hour, semi-structured interviews with fifteen African American, Caribbean American, and West African young women, ages sixteen to twenty-one, who attend or have attended focal high schools and have participated in KAVI. This was a purposive, nonproportional quota

sample of current KAVI Women's Program participants and alum-
nae, reflecting small but representative sample sizes, similar to other
studies of intersectionality and high school–aged urban girls of color
(Ruglis 2011; Wun 2016). These interviews became a Black feminist
praxis (Banks Wallace 2000; Lindsay-Dennis 2015; Lindsay-Dennis,
Cummings, and McClendon 2011)—they opened up space and time
for Black girls to share stories, speak for themselves, name their own
experiences, and theorize about their own lives.

Analysis was guided by a thematic approach (Emerson, Fretz, and
Shaw 2011). Interview text was read first to identify emergent themes.
Emergent themes were initially member-checked in discussions
with the staff from KAVI. I reread interview text to develop detailed
codes and subcodes (Saldaña 2015). Then, Ms. Sutton and Ms. Rivera
reread the transcripts and developed codes and subcodes separately.
To establish inter-rater reliability, all authors met and discussed the
results of their separate analyses, reconciled any inconsistencies, and
agreed upon final themes, codes, subcodes, and related definitions for
the codebook (Merriam 2014). Next, the Dedoose web-based analytical program was used to aid in sorting and management of the qualitative data. Analytic memos were developed that addressed themes,
analytic points, and interpretations of analytic points (Emerson, Fretz,
and Shaw 2011). We also conducted a total of five poetry workshops,
incorporating the method of "participatory narrative analysis" (Dill
2015) in which the participants were introduced to poetic techniques,
poetic forms, and published works of writers of color, such as Patricia
Smith, Vievee Francis, Roger Bonair Agard, Mahogany L. Browne,
and t'ai freedom ford. This helped us to engage in a deeper discussion of ethnicity, gender, sexuality, family, trauma, and resistance in
the girls' lives (Dill, Rivera, and Sutton 2018). KAVI participants then
created *interpretive poems* (Dill 2015; Langer and Furman 2004; Dill,
Rivera, and Sutton 2018), which reveal their own lived experiences

with multiple forms of violence. Through this participatory narrative analysis, participants also provided member checks of the data, themes, and a preliminary analysis, as a way of increasing validity (Dill 2015; Furman et al. 2007).

Findings

The interview excerpts and analytical commentary below contextually illustrate and are representative of key thematic points that emerged during analysis. These excerpts reveal the young women's experiences navigating and articulating their own complex identities.

"I Like What I Like": Disrupting Politics of Respectability

African American, Caribbean American, and West African girls actively disrupt "respectability" politics, such as perceived appropriate feminine attire. Smokey, an eighteen-year-old college freshman, shares, "So, I was with my dad and my brother, so, instead of dresses, I had shorts or whatever. Yeah, so he [my dad] would, like, dress me as a boy, so, like, as I got older, that's just how I continued to dress." Respectability politics are known as the "rules to follow" for marginalized groups, especially young Black women, to be accepted by mainstream society (Higginbotham 1993). These rules govern speech, sexuality, education, and appearance, often dictating what is and what is not considered acceptable. Smokey recognizes that her attire is outside of societal norms, but this does not deter her from staying true to herself.

Black girls also recognize that the politics of decorum vary by gender and age. Jay, another eighteen-year-old college freshman, comments, "Like, my brothers, both of them have a lot of tattoos and she's [my mother] like, 'You guys are the devil.' She insists that it's, like, horrible. 'You should have never done that.' But with me it's like, they had tattoos when they were in the house. She explains that she was unaware. I don't know how that was possible. But if I get a tattoo, she tells me I'll have to leave and she's never going to speak to me ever again." Jay recognizes the double standards inherent in respectability politics.

Additionally, by resisting labels related to sexuality, Black girls further disrupt traditional thought. Fleeky, a seventeen-year-old high school senior, shares,

> LeConté: Um, and do you use titles? Or you like, "I'm bi, I'm gay?"
> Fleeky: No. I'm just me!
> LeConté: Yeah.
> Fleeky: I like what I like.

Fleeky matter-of-factly states that she is just her, marking another instance of the disturbance of the binary concept of sexuality. Black girls exhibit what Diamond (2003) asserts as being comfortable with looking at sexuality as a continuum.

"I'm Smarter Than My Mom Gives Me Credit For": Navigating Complex Mother-Daughter Relationships

Black girls often take on a caregiver role in their families. Rihanna, an eighteen-year-old college freshman, shares, "Now I see how my mom felt when I was that age. When I was tryna find myself. Find my personality. Who I am. I see it in her [my sister] and I'm like, 'Please don't make the wrong mistakes. Please don't make the wrong mistakes.'" Additionally, Rihanna remarks,

> She'll [my mom] get better. She's strong [*chuckle*]. She's a great person. She just needs to learn how to take care of herself. That one thing she

lacks, 110 percent, is taking care of herself. Mainly because she's usually taking care of my little sister and my [older] brother. And me from time to time. But I don't try to depend on her. . . . That's why I work. I have a joint account with my boyfriend for the phone. So, I pay my own phone bill, own Metrocard, hair needs to be done, nails need to be done.

Rihanna takes an active role in caring for her sister, and also in taking care of her mother who is battling several illnesses. She is conscious about not wanting to overburden her mother, so she has a job and pays her own bills. Such consciousness and negotiation of roles and of voice are often amplified in Black immigrant households. Rihanna is Haitian American. Caribbean American and West African girls often negotiate their "gendered diasporas" (Brown 1998) through their complex relationships with their mothers and other family members (Pinnock 2016).

Caribbean American and West African daughters and mothers often oscillate between power struggles and of understanding (Chen 2004). Anti, who is Malian American and a sixteen-year-old high school junior, wrote the following poem in response to Mahogany L. Browne's 2009 list poem "Advice to Rihanna," where she uses Browne's form of dialogue to tease out messages that she hears in her own family:

Mother says: "You never do nothing."
Father says: "Ever since the phones came."
Mother says: "Seriously, she changed."
Father says: "She's the worst out of all of them now."
I say: "What did I do?"
Father says: "You changed drastically."
I say: "How?"
Father says: "You don't read no more. Nothing."

I say: "I never used to read."

Mother says: "Lies!"

Father says "Who you telling?"

Caribbean American and West African girls navigate between pre-conceived "proper" constructs of themselves and those of their African American friends and neighbors (LaBennett 2011). Caribbean American and West African girls actively cultivate and navigate what Pinnock (2016) calls "Diasporic Blackness"—embracing their Afro-Caribbean and West African identities that are not from an oppositional engagement with Blackness and embracing an African American identity. Caribbean and Caribbean American literature actually informs us most saliently about this "Diasporic Blackness" more than social science research has (Mehni 2011). For example, Paule Marshall's novel *Brown Girls, Brownstones* (1959) proposes a sense of selfhood containing multiple nuanced facets.

Jay, who is Grenadian American and Jamaican American, expresses how Caribbean American daughters might experience a lack of trust from their mothers. She comments, "And when she found out I was having sex, she was just like, 'No. I had your sister when I was sixteen and I don't want you having children young.' She gave me that little speech and she was like—I feel like when it comes to that, I'm smarter than my mom gives me credit for." Princess shares,

LeConté: Oh. And your mom's Trini?

Princess: Mm-hmm.

LeConté: And she won't let you go there [to Trinidad]?

Princess: She don't. My father told her, "I'll take her."

LeConté: To Trinidad?

Princess: No, Guyana. My father went, so he's like, "I'll take her." My mother is like, "I don't know." She don't want me to go there because "my daughter is going to be kidnapped; she going to get raped."

LeConté: They grew up there and came here when they were kids or adults?

Princess: No, my father's family; my father's been here.

LeConté: And your mom?

Princess: My mother—she so scared of everything.

LeConté: But where did she grow up? Here?

Princess: Yeah.

LeConté: Oh, but her family is from Trinidad?

Princess: Yeah.

LeConté: So, she didn't like—it's not like she grew up there and she knows how it is. She's just scared?

Princess: She's scared. Cuz, she's like, "I heard so much stuff about it."

Most of the mother's concerns, frustrations, and restrictions, and therefore clashes with their daughters, are around perceptions and fears around their daughters' sexual activity, sexuality, and threats of sexual assault. The protagonist in *Brown Girls, Brownstones*, Selina, like many of our participants, experiences her family and her community as both a completion of herself and as a source of control and constraint in her life (Jones 1998). Caribbean American daughters and mothers share a bond that is not exclusive to contention. Selina, like our participants, works to "be her own woman in her mother's presence" (Chen 2004, 258). Black girls in our study sit within this tension, as well.

"My Loyalty Is So Real": Fierce Loyalty to Family and Friends

Loyalty among Black girls can often stir up intense emotions. In the following excerpt, Fleeky shares, "Because it was, like, I don't know, I would stick up for my friends. Like, my loyalty is so—is so real. I don't know, it just got me so upset, like, so very angry. So, I just reacted but now, I thought about it." Black girls defend these "loyalty links" (Dill and Ozer 2016; Jones 2009) through fighting alongside friends and/

or fighting for the maintenance of their friendships. Much of their conversation around fighting also has to do with safety. Black girls use texting and social media as a way to communicate about safety to their friends. Princess comments, "I told them—I dead asked them, 'Please, do not go to school on Friday because I'm not going to be able to be there.' I was on FaceTime with them and they was crazy. They all standing there. Her cousins in the car [ready to fight]. I'm just like, 'Why all of this when I'm not here? Why?'" Princess feels obligated to protect her friends during an imminent fight, which she tried to warn them about through texting and FaceTime, and she feels guilt for not being there to physically protect or defend them. Black girls work to establish loyalty and trust through the creation of signals aided by social media and technology. According to Dill and Ozer (2016), youth believe that they are obligated to defend and protect their friends in conflict. Sharing passwords through social media accounts is another way in which Black girls demonstrate their loyalty. Purple, a seventeen-year-old high school senior, comments, "She asked—she inboxed me to ask about someone's relationship and I told her. And that person had my password and was talking to her. And she is mad at me because the person was talking to her." This excerpt also shows how disloyalty can influence the cycle of Black girls' friendships. Nico, a seventeen-year-old high school junior, shares,

> She went and told the girl my business. So, I was like, "Obviously, you're not my friend." And asked her why she did it. She said, "Oh, because, he's lying to her." So, I felt like her loyalty was more to the other girl than it was to me, so I was like, "Obviously, I can't trust you. You're not somebody that I need as a friend." There was no beef or nothing. I just let it go. I stopped talking to her. We just stay out of each other's way.

In addition to defending friendships, Black girls note the ways in which they defend their family. Rihanna shares, "They didn't expect us to react that way. But no, honey. Nuh-mmm. Not my cousin [*laughing*]. And I just remember, like, at the end, like, after everybody was separated, I was like, 'WHERE'S MY COUSIN?! WHERE'S MY COUSIN?!' Like, I would not relax until I saw her." Even if they do not self-identify as *fighters*, Black girls protect their #squad, including their family and friends, fiercely and loyally (Jones 2009).

"I Can Only Do Me": Subsistence Through Activating One's Own Internal Resources

Black girls also rely on emotional and communal support as a survival strategy. Tayla, a twenty-one-year-old college sophomore, shares, "And I feel like in KAVI, I did start that transformation. Like, it really did. Also, in talking with [KAVI facilitator], I feel like she knew that I—like, she saw the bigger picture for me. Even though I would be sitting there talking about weed, she'd be like, 'What?' But she kinda— she never judged me because she could see that I could grow out of it." Black girls reach out to adult mentors and others for support. However, they also resist perceived labels of deficiency that adults in their lives may put upon them. Smokey remarks, "I wouldn't say [I was] traumatized. I mean, the doctor says 'traumatized.' And I was supposed to go see a therapist. But I'm like, I don't believe in therapy, so. . . . It was, like, the thing that my, um, mom, had—the accident. So, I was there. I wouldn't say 'traumatized.' I would say I was paralyzed in the moment. I guess how I dealt with it after that. Was I traumatized? I'm not sure. But I don't really think so." Smokey goes on to share, "It's like, I feel like people are so temporary. So, it's like, why am I going to sit here and argue over something and you're probably not going to be here a couple months from now? Like, you know what I mean? Like, it don't make sense. But, um, people don't have the same mindset as me. So, whatever." Black girls work to create and activate their own "survival strategies" (Jones 2009; Lindsay-Dennis 2015). They are self-reflective about their past experiences, their familal and social relationships.

After reading Mahogany L. Browne's 2015 poem "TO DO LIST," which narrates what the protagonist can or cannot do, Alexandra, a seventeen-year-old high school senior wrote,

I can only smile
I can only love
I can only give back
I can only care
I can only cry
I can only hurt
I can only take enough
I can never give up
I can only do me!

"Doing me" is ultimately a form of Black girls' self-care strategies. Black girls also cultivate their survival through dialogue and creative writing. Our participants activate healing (Dill, Rivera, and Sutton 2018) through their practice of reading, writing, and sharing poetry. Ruth Nicole Brown (2013) similarly details how such praxes create a sense of hopefulness and future orientation for Black girls, even in the face of distress,

Because my story
is hers
hers is mine
what does it mean for me to tell our story? (2013, 140)

These resources can provide "instrumental and emotional support," which, according to Yosso (2005), aids in the navigation of oppressive institutions, and also in the navigation of growing up.

Conclusion

Walk in your ways so you won't crumble (so you won't crumble)
Walk in your ways so you can sleep at night
Walk in your ways so you can wake up and rise
—SOLANGE KNOWLES, "RISE"

Our findings reveal that Black girls navigate and articulate their own complex identities. This reliance on their own personal power amidst trials and triumph, while being in community with their family members and building sisterhood with other Black girls, is their activation of #BlackGirlMagic. #BlackGirlMagic is often bidirectional or multidirectional. For example, the young women in our study enlighten and inspire us as adult women with their strategies of self-articulation. As we strive to be "worthy witnesses" (Winn and Ubiles 2011) in Black girls' lives, we strive to be our full selves so that they see us in our ordinariness, not just in a sometimes abstract and intangible extra-ordinariness. We ask critical questions of the girls in KAVI workshops and in research interviews, holding them in their introspection, and, in turn, they do the same with us.

Our participants enact #BlackGirlMagic using four common practices. First, they work to disrupt respectability politics. Second, Caribbean American and West African girls further "shapeshift" (Cox 2015) through their creation of transnational identities of "Diasporic Blackness" (Pinnock 2016). Third, Black girls are fiercely loyal to their family and friends. Lastly, Black girls ultimately draw upon their own internal resources as they subsist and conceive of their own future identities, opportunities, and experiences. In this way, Black girls activate Black feminism's centering of identifying and engaging in coping mechanisms (Collins 1990). Ultimately, Black girls work hard to take care of themselves and their cherished loved ones. Black girls work hard to rise and to continue rising.

Acknowledgments

Our deepest appreciation to the young women in KAVI, whose insights and experiences made this work possible. We also thank the following KAVI staff and interns: Dr. Robert Gore, Elizabeth Ige, Sharena Soutar-Frith, Jacquel Clemons, Shaquasha Shannon, Christine Hollingsworth, Lizzie DeWan, Dr. Tosin Ojugbele, Shanna-Kay Townsend, Britany Thomas, and Alecia Johnson.

FUNDING: This study is supported by the Kaiser Permanente Burch Minority Leadership Development Program and the SUNY Downstate Medical Center's President's Health Disparities Grant.

Note

1.   All names used are pseudonyms, selected by the participants.

Works Cited

Bambara, Toni Cade, ed. 1970. *The Black Woman: An Anthology*. New York: New American Library.

Banks-Wallace, JoAnne. 2000. "Womanist Ways of Knowing: Theoretical Considerations for Research with African American Women." *Advances in Nursing Science* 22 (3): 33–45.

Brown, Jacqueline Nassy. 1998. "Black Liverpool, Black America, and the Gendering of Diasporic Space." *Cultural Anthropology* 13 (3): 291–325.

Brown, Ruth Nicole. 2007. "Remembering Maleesa: Theorizing Black Girl Politics and the Politicizing of Socialization." *National Political Science Review* 11: 121–36.

Brown, Ruth Nicole. 2013. *Hear Our Truths: The Creative Potential of Black Girlhood*. Champaign: University of Illinois Press.

Browne, Mahogany L. 2009. *Advice to Rihanna*. Nuyorican Poets Café. YouTube. August 18.

Browne, Mahogany L. 2015. "TO DO LIST." *RedBone*. Detroit, Mich.: Willow Books.

Burton, Linda M. 1997. "Ethnography and the Meaning of Adolescence in High-Risk Neighborhoods." *Ethos* 25 (2): 208–17.

Chen, Shu-Ling. 2004. "Journey to Be Her Own Selina: Broadening Ethnic Boundary for Selfhood in Marshall." *Dong Hwa Journal of Humanities* 6: 255–89.

Collins, Patricia Hill. 1990. *Black Feminist Thought: Knowledge, Consciousness, and the Politics of Empowerment*. Boston: Unwin Hyman.

Combahee River Collective. 2000. "A Black Feminist Statement (1977)." In *The Black Feminist Reader*, ed. Joy James and Tracy Denean Sharpley-Whiting, 261–70. Malden, Mass.: Blackwell.

Cox, Aimee Meredith. 2015. *Shapeshifters: Black Girls and the Choreography of Citizenship*. Durham, N.C.: Duke University Press.

Crenshaw, Kimberlé. 1991. "Mapping the Margins: Intersectionality, Identity Politics, and Violence against Women of Color." *Stanford Law Review* 43: 1241–99.

Development Services Group Inc. 2013. *Protective Factors for Populations Served by the Administration on Children, Youth, and Families: A Literature Review and Theoretical Framework*. Report submitted to Office on Child Abuse and Neglect. Children's Bureau. Administration on Children, Youth, and Families, Washington, D.C. http://www.dsgonline.com/acyf/DSG%20Protective%20Factors%20Literature%20Review%202013.pdf.

Diamond, Lisa M. 2003. "Was It a Phase? Young Women's Relinquishment of Lesbian/Bisexual Identities over a 5-Year Period." *Journal of Personality and Social Psychology* 84 (2): 352–64.

Dill, LeConté J. 2015. "Poetic Justice: Engaging in Participatory Narrative Analysis to Find Solace in the 'Killer Corridor.'" *American Journal of Community Psychology* 55 (1–2): 128–35.

Dill, LeConté J., and Emily J. Ozer. 2016. "'I'm Not Just Runnin' the Streets': Exposure to Neighborhood Violence and Violence Management Strategies Among Urban Youth of Color." *Journal of Adolescent Research* 31 (5): 536–56. https://doi.org/0743558415605382.

Dill, LeConté J., Bianca Rivera, and Shavaun Sutton. 2018. "'Don't Let Nobody Bring You Down': How Urban Black Girls Write and Learn from Ethnographically-based Poetry to Understand and Heal from Relationship Violence." *Ethnographic Edge* 2 (1): 57–65.

Elwood, Sarah A., and Deborah G. Martin. 2000. "'Placing' Interviews: Location and Scales of Power in Qualitative Research." *Professional Geographer* 52 (4): 649–57.

Emerson, Robert M., Rachel I. Fretz, and Linda L. Shaw. 2011. *Writing Ethnographic Fieldnotes*. Chicago: University of Chicago Press.

Few, April L., Dionne P. Stephens, and Marlo Rouse-Arnett. 2003. "Sister-to-Sister Talk: Transcending Boundaries and Challenges in Qualitative Research with Black Women." *Family Relations* 52 (3): 205–15.

Furman, Rich, Carol L. Langer, Christine S. Davis, Heather P. Gallardo, and Shanti Kulkarni. 2007. "Expressive, Research and Reflective Poetry as Qualitative Inquiry: A Study of Adolescent Identity." *Qualitative Research* 7 (3): 301–15.

Gaunt, Kyra D. 2006. *The Games Black Girls Play: Learning the Ropes from Double-Dutch to Hip-Hop*. New York: New York University Press.

Higginbotham, Evelyn Brooks. 1993. *Righteous Discontent: The Women's Movement in the Black Baptist Church, 1880–1920*. Cambridge, Mass.: Harvard University Press.

Jones, Gavin. 1998. "'The Sea Ain't Got No Back Door': The Problems of Black Consciousness in Paule Marshall's *Brown Girl, Brownstones*." *African American Review* 32 (4): 597–606.

Jones, Nikki. 2009. *Between Good and Ghetto*. New Brunswick, N.J.: Rutgers University Press.

Knowles, Solange, Raymond Angry, Troy Johnson, Ahmir Khalib Thompson, Devon Welsh, and Raphael Saadiq. Solange Knowles, vocalist. 2016. "Rise." Audio. On *A Seat at the Table*. EMI April Music Inc, Sony/ATV Music Publishing LLC, Kobalt Music Publishing Ltd.

Koonce, Jacqueline B. 2012. "'Oh Those Loud Black Girls!': A Phenomenological Study of Black Girls Talking with an Attitude." *Journal of Language and Literacy Education* 8 (2): 26–46.

LaBennett, Oneka. 2011. *She's Mad Real: Popular Culture and West Indian Girls in Brooklyn*. New York: New York University Press.

Ladner, Joyce. 1971. *Tomorrow's Tomorrow: The Black Woman*. Garden City, N.Y.: Doubleday.

Langer, Carol L., and Rich Furman. 2004. "Exploring Identity and Assimilation: Research and Interpretive Poems." *Forum: Qualitative Social Research* 5 (2). http://dx.doi.org/10.17169/fqs-5.2.609.

Lindsay-Dennis, LaShawnda. 2015. "Black Feminist-Womanist Research Paradigm: Toward a Culturally Relevant Research Model Focused on African American Girls." *Journal of Black Studies* 46 (5): 506–20.

Lindsay-Dennis, LaShawnda, Lawanda Cummings, and Susan Crim McClendon. 2011. "Mentors' Reflections on Developing a Culturally Responsive Mentoring Initiative for Urban African American Girls." *Black Women, Gender, and Families* 5 (2): 66–92.

Love, Bettina L. 2012. *Hip Hop's Li'l Sistas Speak: Negotiating Hip Hop Identities and Politics in the New South*. New York: Peter Lang.

Marshall, Paule. 1959. *Brown Girls, Brownstones*. New York: Feminist Press.

Mehni, Masoumeh. 2011. "Analyzing the Problematic Mother-Daughter Relationship in Edwidge Danticat's 'Breath, Eyes, Memory.'" *Journal of Caribbean Literatures* 7 (1): 77–90.

Merriam, Sharan B. 2014. *Qualitative Research: A Guide to Design and Implementation*. San Francisco, Calif.: John Wiley and Sons.

Morris, Edward W. 2007. "'Ladies' or 'Loudies'? Perceptions and Experiences of Black Girls in Classrooms." *Youth and Society* 38 (4): 490–515.

Nespor, Jan. 2000. "Anonymity and Place in Qualitative Inquiry." *Qualitative Inquiry* 6 (4): 546–69.

Pinnock, Christine A. 2016. "A Means to An End: Articulations of Diasporic Blackness, Class and Survival among Female Afro-Caribbean Service Workers in New York City." PhD diss., City University of New York.

Pyscher, Tracey, and Brian D. Lozenski. 2014. "Throwaway Youth: The Sociocultural Location of Resistance to Schooling." *Equity and Excellence in Education* 47 (4): 531–45.

Ruglis, Jessica. 2011. "Mapping the Biopolitics of School Dropout and Youth Resistance." *International Journal of Qualitative Studies in Education* 24 (5): 627–37.

Saldaña, Johnny. 2015. *The Coding Manual for Qualitative Researchers*. Thousand Oaks, Calif.: SAGE.

Sampson, Robert J., and Stephen W. Raudenbush. 1999. "Systematic Social Observation of Public Spaces: A New Look at Disorder in Urban Neighborhoods." *American Journal of Sociology* 105 (3): 603–51.

Stephens, Dionne P., and Layli D. Phillips. 2003. "Freaks, Gold Diggers, Divas, and Dykes: The Sociohistorical Development of Adolescent African American Women's Sexual Scripts." *Sexuality and Culture* 7 (1): 3–49.

Stewart, Maria W., and Marilyn Richardson. 1987. *Maria W. Stewart, America's First Black Woman Political Writer: Essays and Speeches*. Bloomington: Indiana University Press.

Thomson, Denise, Lana Bzdel, Karen Golden-Biddle, Trish Reay, and Carole A. Estabrooks. 2005. "Central Questions of Anonymization: A Case Study of Secondary Use of Qualitative Data." *Forum Qualitative Sozialforschung/Forum: Qualitative Social Research* 6 (1). doi: http://dx.doi.org/10.17169/fqs-6.1.511.

Winn, Maisha T. 2011. *Girl Time: Literacy, Justice, and the School-to-Prison Pipeline*. New York: Teachers College Press.

Winn, Maisha T., and Joseph R. Ubiles. 2011. "Worthy Witnessing: Collaborative Research in Urban Classrooms." In *Studying Diversity in Teacher Education*, edited by Arnetha F. Ball and Cynthia A. Tyson, 295–308. New York: Rowman and Littlefield.

Wun, Connie. 2016. "Against Captivity: Black Girls and School Discipline Policies in the Afterlife of Slavery." *Educational Policy* 30 (1): 171–96.

Yosso, Tara J. 2005. "Whose Culture Has Capital? A Critical Race Theory Discussion of Community Cultural Wealth." *Race Ethnicity and Education* 8 (1): 69–91.

CHAPTER 3

IDENTITY IN FORMATION

Black Girl Critical Literacies in Independent Schools

Charlotte E. Jacobs

Introduction

Well, to answer the first question, [what identities do you think about most often?], I would definitely say being a Black female is an identifier. I think about sports a lot . . . soccer. I play soccer, but I've stopped playing basketball and I feel at Grace [the name of her school] sometimes since you're Black, people think, "Oh, if you're Black, you like basketball." And it's true, I like basketball, but I'm not—I don't play or anything. I feel like what you do shouldn't have anything to do with what you look like—and then, identities I think about the least often, probably grades and, like, grades, yeah. Even though schoolwork should be number one, and I think about it a lot, but then people don't look at you for what you do, they look at you for what you look like, and that's kind of not cool.

—JENNIFER,[1] TENTH GRADER

In the excerpt above, Jennifer is sharing with a group of fifteen high-school-aged Black girls the identity map she created as part of a weekly discussion group for high school Black girls who attend independent schools.[2] Jennifer is a "lifer" at her school, meaning that she has attended her independent school since she was in prekindergarten. Jennifer's awareness of her identity of what it means to be a Black girl; her assessment of her stereotyped status of being a basketball player at her elite, predominantly white independent school; and her critique of the messages that students and teachers at her school seem to communicate about what attributes and personal characteristics are valued are examples of an emergent concept that I have developed called *Black girl critical literacies* (BGCL).

I define BGCL as the phenomenon in which Black girls use particular competencies to recognize, process, and respond to messages that they receive connected to their status as Black adolescent girls in U.S. society while simultaneously crafting their own sense of their Black girl identities. My decision to use the concept of BGCL to study the experiences of Black girls in independent schools speaks to not only *what* their experiences are but also *how* Black girls understand and critically view their experiences. I envision that the ways in which Black girls enact BGCL serve as a form of BlackGirlMagic in that they are using particular skills and strategies not only to critique their experiences as Black girls in the United States but also a call to action to disrupt the oppressive systems of which they are a part. Through BGCL, Black girls enact BlackGirlMagic by learning how to fearlessly define who they are for themselves in the face of being defined by others.

This chapter explores the experiences of Black girls who attend elite, predominantly white independent schools; a subpopulation of Black girls whose academic, social, and emotional experiences in school continue to remain outside of academic conversations focusing on Black girls and education. In response to the current trend of Black girls' negative educational experiences and often poor career and life outcomes for those who attend under-resourced public schools in the United States, Black parents are increasingly searching for alternatives to their children's education in traditional public schools (Slaughter-Defoe et al. 2012). Independent schools, known for their access to resources (Slaughter-Defoe et al. 2012), promotion of a rigorous curriculum (Slaughter-Defoe et al. 2012), and prestigious alumni career trajectories and leadership networks (Domhoff 2005; Karabel 2006), serve as a viable option for many Black parents who view education as the key to social mobility in the United States (Slaughter-Defoe et al. 2012).

While independent schools are touted as sites of social mobility, they are also institutions whose historical roots are grounded in the ideology of social, financial, and racial exclusion and inaccessibility (Gaztambide-Fernández 2009). Though these schools have become increasingly diverse, the reality is that as of the 2017–18 school year, the average student population comprised of roughly 6.8 percent African American, 5 percent Latino, 8.5 percent Asian American, 8.5 percent multiracial American, 0.5 percent Native American, 0.8 percent Pacific Islander, 1.8 percent Middle Eastern, and 62.9 percent European American students (National Association of Independent Schools [NAIS] 2016). In terms of socioeconomic diversity, the average tuition of NAIS member schools was $23,963 per year for day schools and between $42,000 and $56,071 for boarding schools. Relatedly, an average of 23.7 percent of students who attend independent schools receive financial assistance from the school (NAIS 2016).

This chapter presents the experiences of those students who do not embody the average demographics of an independent school student. I argue that the racial, gender, and sometimes socioeconomic identities of Black girls who attend independent schools classify them as a racialized and gendered "other" (hooks 1990) within their elite, predominantly white school environment, and that this othered status leads to the development of particular strategies that support them in processing encounters of race, gender, and class in relation to the crafting of their adolescent Black girl identities.

The othered status of Black girls in independent schools exists not only at the level of school population demographics but is also reflected in the lack of attention that scholars have dedicated to researching their particular experiences in school. Similar to the trend of social

science research concerning Black girls in education, the experiences of Black girls in independent schools are often subsumed within
research that describes the general experiences of Black youth who
attend independent schools (Slaughter-Defoe et al. 2012). The limited
research that explores the experiences of Black girls in independent
schools tends to focus on the influence of the school environment *on*
Black girls (Alexander-Snow 1999; Horvat and Antonio 1999), creating
a situation where they are solely *receivers* of messages related to race or
ethnicity, gender, and socioeconomic status, ignoring the *agency* that
Black girls have in constructing their own sense of identity.

In this chapter, I will first present an overview of the existing
research about Black girls' experiences in independent schools, then
I will describe the theories that serve as guideposts for a preliminary
theory of BGCL. Next, I will present how BGCL is situated within the
context of independent schools by describing each component of the
theory and how they are related to one another. As I present the preliminary theory, I will show how the Black girls who participated in
a four-month study that included weekly discussion groups and one-
on-one interviews embodied each aspect of the BGCL model.[3] I will
close the chapter by discussing the implications of a BGCL model for
educators, practitioners, and researchers in the service of supporting
the positive development of adolescent Black girls and their enact-
ment of BlackGirlMagic.

Reviewing the Literature: Black Girls' Experiences in Independent Schools

The seminal works of Diana T. Slaughter and Deborah J. Johnson
(1988) and Lorene Cary (1991) and the ethnographic studies of Mia
Alexander-Snow (1999) and Erin McNamara Horvat and Anthony
Lising Antonio (1999) offer a picture where Black girls are often the

"outsiders within" (Collins 1986) their elite, predominantly white schools. In this circumstance, Black girls' intersecting identities of being Black, female, and of differing socioeconomic backgrounds often push them to the margins of academic and social circles in their daily school environments. Yet, even as outsiders, paradoxically, Black girls still have access to a privileged world of resources and networks that are not open to many people. Common themes of Black girls' academic, social, and emotional experiences in independent schools seem to persist throughout time and across different types of independent schools (boarding vs. day, single-sex vs. coed, rural vs. urban). Academically, Black girls often experience microaggressions (Sue et al. 2007) in the form of teachers and peers questioning their academic abilities by assuming that they received admission to the school solely through affirmative action-related policies and not by merit (White 2013). Relatedly, Black girls in this study and in other research studies described experiences where their teachers either expressed surprise or doubted that they were capable of being successful in honors and advanced courses (White 2013).

In the social arena, the overall experience for Black girls is a narrative of constantly trying to fit into a school culture that was not made for them. From their schools, which serve as sites of societal reproduction (Bowles and Gintis 1976), they receive messages that their identities of race, gender, and often socioeconomic status intersect to exclude them from what is valued in society—they are not boys; they do not embody white feminine beauty standards of having straight hair, light skin, and thin figures; and their class status could also place them outside of middle-class norms (Hill 2002; Jones 2015; Ward 1990). In juxtaposition to their status as being outside of the norm, the literature also reflects how Black girls are often only valued socially because they are seen as being "cool" by their white peers and as experts on Black culture and slang—often stemming from the assumption that all Black girls live in the "ghetto" or the "hood" (Alexander-Snow 1999; White 2013). In response to their out-sider status in relation to their white peers, the literature also shows how Black girls in independent schools often create their own affinity groups, whether formally or informally, as a way to find sources of affirmation, understanding, and solidarity (Chase 2008; Gaztambide-Fernández and DiAquoi 2010; White 2013).

Emotionally, Black girls in independent schools, similar to Black girls in public schools, often experience policing and management of their emotions by administrators, teachers, and peers (Chase 2008; Horvat and Antonio 1999). Scholars have found that educators often hold a particular bias that Black girls need more social correction than other student subpopulations, and therefore their behaviors and actions fall under intense scrutiny because they do not resem-ble accepted institutional norms, which usually stem from a white normative frame (Evans-Winters and Esposito 2010; Gibson 2015). Growing research on Black girls' experiences in school shows that Black girls in various types of school, be it predominantly students of color or predominantly white, are often viewed by their teachers and administrators as loud, unruly, disrespectful, and unmanageable, when, typically, the situation was that Black girls were attempting to express their opinions and needs (Evans-Winters and Girls for Gen-der Equality 2017; Morris 2007).

Theoretical Underpinnings of BGCL

The concept of BGCL draws on Black feminist-inspired and devel-opmental theories in order to situate the experiences of Black girls in schools as a result of their intersecting, oppressed identities of being young, Black, and girls in the United States, and what competencies and strategies they employ when experiencing encounters of race, gender, and class.

Black Girlhood

Black girlhood is an asset-oriented framework that emphasizes the agency, creativity, and resistance of Black girls (Brown 2013). Based on her qualitative research with adolescent Black girls, Ruth Nicole Brown developed five principles that characterize the Black girlhood framework: (1) articulate visionary Black girlhood as a meaningful practice, (2) showcase Black girl inventiveness of form and content, (3) expand our vision of Black girlhood beyond identity, (4) sense radical courage and interdependence, and (5) honor praxis, the analytical insight that comes only by way of consistent action and reflection (2013, 3).

Another element of Brown's Black girlhood framework is that it can be used as an organizing framework in order to encourage and move Black girls toward the collective action of critiquing their status in the United States. Brown emphasizes the presence and importance of the knowledge that Black girls possess, and also focuses on Black girls as agents rather than objects within systems of power in our society. Brown's Black girlhood framework articulates the potential for Black girls to come together to create change when they take a critical stance toward the ways in which they are positioned, degraded, and oftentimes ignored in society.

Racial Literacy

Emerging from the areas of racial and ethnic socialization and coping strategies within the field of psychology, Stevenson defines racial literacy as "the ability to read, recast, and resolve racially stressful social interactions" (2014). Based on his work with Black boys over the timespan of two decades, Stevenson's theory of racial literacy acknowledges the stress that often emerges when one is involved in a racial encounter. Due to the significant role that race plays in society, almost any encounter or experience in which race is involved will create a certain amount of stress to which one must respond. Stevenson asserts that learning how to effectively cope with and respond to these encounters is essential to the healthy development of Black boys. In this chapter, I build on the concept of racial literacy and expand it to describe how Black girls recognize, process, and respond to interactions that arise as a result of their being Black girls in the United States, and particularly within independent schools.

Toward a Theory of Black Girl Critical Literacies in Independent Schools

The preliminary theory of BGCL emerged from my work with Black girls in grades nine through twelve at two different independent school sites located in the suburbs just outside of an urban center in the northeastern part of the United States. There were ten to fifteen girls at each site. They represented a wide range of experiences based on the number of years they had attended their school (a third had been in the school since kindergarten, a third entered in middle school, and a third entered in high school), socioeconomic background, and academic standing. Seven of the of the participants were part of a qualitative study that I conducted previously at one of the school sites for a two-year span that explored the raced and gendered experiences of middle school Black girls in independent schools. At the time of that study, the girls were in sixth, seventh, and eighth grade.

Over a period of four months, the girls participated in a weekly discussion group where they discussed their experiences as Black girls in their school, in their communities, and in larger society. The weekly discussion groups contained discussion prompts that drew on themes of Black feminism (Collins 2000), intersectionality (Crenshaw 1991), and the cycle of oppression (Bishop 2002). The weekly sessions also included activities such as identity mapping, watching videos and news clips, and brainstorming sessions around changes the participants wanted to see in their schools. As part of the study, the girls completed pre- and post-questionnaires that explored how they were defining and recognizing experiences of racism, sexism, and classism, and more than half of the girls also participated in one-on-one interviews (see the appendix for an abbreviated version of the questionnaires).[4]

Through the use of a grounded theory methodology I was able to identify and understand the emergent components of BGCL and how they relate to each other in order to explain how Black girls navigate through their daily school lives and construct their identities. Figure 3.1 illustrates how I conceptualize BGCL in independent schools in action.

The Influence of School Culture

In this model, school culture functions as the overarching landscape in which BGCL takes place. I found that the majority of what study participants thought, said, and expressed could be understood through the context of their school culture, which were elite, predominantly white spaces. As figure 3.1 illustrates, school culture mediates each element of the BGCL action and interaction cycle, which in turn influences the entire process of BGCL. According to Mikie Loughridge and Loren R. Tarantino (2004), school culture can be comprised of the following elements: heroes and heroines; communication networks; rites and rituals; lore and myths; rules, rewards, and sanctions; and physical environment. These components of school culture all influence the raced, gendered, and classed experiences that Black girls have in independent schools by communicating messages to them of what ways of thinking, being, and feeling are valued, who belongs and who is left out of the school culture, and what the power dynamics are within the school space.

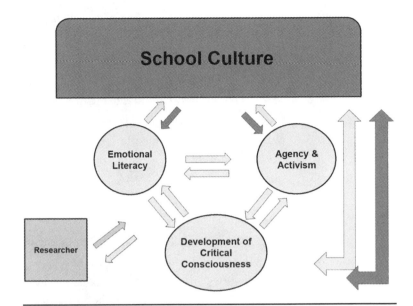

FIGURE 3.1 A preliminary theory of Black girl critical literacies in independent schools.

Another aspect of this model is how school culture itself can be influenced by the emotional literacy, actions, and critical awareness of Black girls. The double arrows between school culture and the components of BGCL reflect the reciprocal relationship between context and individuals, with the context of school culture having a larger influence on Black girls than Black girls being able to influence school culture.

The Action and/or Interaction Cycle of the Components of BGCL

The core of the BGCL phenomenon occurs within an action and/or interaction cycle (Corbin and Strauss 2015), where the social and psychological processes of BGCL interact with and react to one another.

The three elements of the BGCL action and/or interaction cycle are a developing critical consciousness, emotional literacy, and agency and activism. Each feed into one another to reflect that BGCL is an ongoing and flexible process that functions in response to the encounters that Black girls experience in their schools. Central to the functioning of this action and interaction cycle is that it can begin at any point of the cycle with the overall outcome remaining the same in terms of how a Black girl chooses to respond to an encounter of race, gender, or class while in school.

A DEVELOPING CRITICAL CONSCIOUSNESS

Drawing on the work of Paulo Freire (2000), this component of BGCL describes the growing awareness that Black girls have about how social relations and identities operate within the larger context of power relations, and how they, as individuals and as a group, are situated within those contexts. Particular to the construction of their identities as Black adolescent girls, critical consciousness takes the form of the understanding that Black girls have about what it means to possess the intersectional identity of being Black girls in their elite, predominantly white school environment as well as in the United States, a development of what Patricia Hill Collins (2000) describes as a "Black women's consciousness." In the example below, during a whole group discussion, Adrienne, an eleventh grader, comments on the privilege that the white students at her school have about not having to talk about race, while race and racism are part of ongoing conversations that Black girls have with each other in her school:

> Wait. I wish you'd talk with your friends about racism and discrimination against Black people. Hashtag all we talk about. It's sad. We shouldn't have to talk about it all the time. That shouldn't be the only thing we talk about. Yes, we talk about other stuff. Silly stuff, but it's majority this. Because this is our every day and the fact that we have to

deal with it here, where I spend exactly twelve hours out of a twenty-four-hour day.

An element of this developing critical consciousness is not only the awareness that Black girls have about how power and privilege operate in society, but also how Black girls use that awareness to analyze and critique their experiences. The extent to which the girls critique traditions, racial demographics, and practices in their schools serve as examples of the interaction between the components of the development of critical consciousness and school culture.

As figure 3.1 shows, the component of *a developing critical consciousness* also interacts with the other BGCL components in a reciprocal way. The level of awareness that Black girls have about their social location in their school and in society can lead to them experiencing certain emotions and/or cause girls to exert their agency in ways that result in different forms of action.

ENGAGING IN EMOTIONAL LITERACY

Stemming from the literature on emotional intelligence (Goleman 2006), the *emotional literacy* component operates on both an internal and external level. On an internal level, this component describes the awareness that Black girls have of their own emotions and the decisions they make to display those emotions. Being able to trace the origins of their emotions during a particular encounter and developing the skills to regulate their emotions is critical to an emerging literacy about how one feels at any given time.

On an external level, similar to critical consciousness, this component reflects Black girls' awareness of how their emotions might be viewed by others because of the stereotypes associated with Black girls and women. Emotional literacy also requires that Black girls are able to read others' emotions. This aspect of emotional literacy is particularly important as Black girls make decisions about when and how to respond to encounters of race, gender, and class within the context of their school culture, which has its own rules and norms about which emotions are allowed to be made visible and how they are allowed to be enacted. In the example below from an individual interview, Tanya, a twelfth grader, reflects on her emotions around anger when she was younger:

> I know I've matured a lot. Even if it's just in high school it's sort of like I've matured a lot because in freshman year, huh, I was like a ticking time bomb, like, I was bad, bad . . . it was the littlest things could just set me off my temp—yeah, that's—my temper in ninth grade was terrible. I [*sigh*] would, like, little things, like, you bump into me and don't want to say excuse me, like that—I would just go off, I could be going off for days. . . . I just remember ninth grade just wasn't my—my time when I just wasn't mature enough, but then I'm in ninth grade; I'm fifteen, fourteen to fifteen years old; I wasn't—I didn't understand that I can't just go off at any time; I just can't do that, and that I had to control myself, but now, I'm a lot better. . . . Yeah, I still get angry but less, like, little—it's little things affecting me when I was in ninth grade, but now the little things, oh, it is okay, I guess, like, move on, even some of the big things, like, after a few days or I don't—see I don't snap anymore as much as I do—did. But after a day or two, I'm over it. Before I could be on that topic for a week, two weeks, a month, and now, a day, I give it a day and a half, I'm over it. It is what it is; life goes on. No one is ever going to stop me from doing anything—hum, yeah, I was crazy, you know? Tanya's a crazy little child.

Tanya's assessment of her past behavior of being similar to a "ticking time bomb" and how she learned over the years that she could not "just go off at any time" illustrates her developing emotional literacy around feelings and displays of anger. Following the tenets of emotional literacy, Tanya displays her emotional literacy on an internal level by identifying her feelings of anger and how she chose to communicate those feelings to others. Though she does not describe the external factors in detail, Tanya's reflection of how she came to understand that she had to find more effective ways of expressing her anger in order to not have any one "stop me from doing anything" demonstrates her awareness of how others may have reacted to her anger.

DISPLAYING BLACK GIRL AGENCY AND ACTIVISM

The *agency and activism* component explores how critical consciousness and awareness interact to influence the decisions and actions that Black girls make when involved in encounters around race, gender, and class. In particular, this component describes the agency that Black girls use to define themselves in the face of being defined by others on a daily basis, as well as the methods that Black girls use to advocate for themselves and for the equity of Black girls and women. In an excerpt from an individual interview below, Renée, a twelfth grader, describes how taking on the identity of a feminist means not tolerating sexist comments from her peers or her friends:

> But I think, yeah, as we've grown now that we just learned not to tolerate such actions; that's not acceptable, and it's not acceptable here. And, I guess, just women in general I think have to take that stand and just be verbal; if something makes you uncomfortable, you need to say something because I sure will not tolerate that kind of talk. And I think this year, being in Gender [referring to her class on gender], that's also empowered so many women, and I don't know there's been talk about that because I remember joining it [her class on gender], and my friend would be like, "Oh my god, you're going to be like one of those annoying feminists," and I was like, "Whoa, what are you talking about?" And I'm like, "You know, do you know the definition of feminism?" [*laughs*]

As figure 3.1 illustrates, Black girls' agency and activism are influenced by their recognition of their emotions and how those emotions contribute toward action and/or inaction. Similarly, the development of critical consciousness influences how Black girls recognize and understand raced, gendered, and classed encounters, and the methods they choose to achieve a particular goal focused on self-definition, resistance, or creating change.

Another aspect of this preliminary theory is that it shows how the context of *school culture* and the component of *activism and agency* interact, with agency and activism having the potential to shift or change aspects of school culture by raising awareness of the experiences of Black girls in school. In the other direction, school culture functions as either a source of promotion or constraint by determining the extent to which Black girls are allowed to express their agency and what forms of activism are deemed appropriate within school culture.

The Influence of the Researcher

Outside of the action and/or interaction cycle, but still a part of the BGCL phenomenon within the context of this study, is the role that I played throughout my time with the participants. Taking a feminist (hooks 2014) and critical pedagogical (McLaren 2015) stance, I positioned the girls as experts of their own lived experiences so that our relationship took on a reciprocal exchange, with each of us serving as teachers and students at different points of our meetings. Throughout the project, I shifted between the roles of researcher, educator and/ or facilitator, and ally—all roles that influence the development of BGCL. As a researcher, I administered pre- and postquestionnaires, developed a curriculum, and conducted interviews that all addressed themes of feminism, racism, sexism, and classism. As an educator and/ or facilitator, I led weekly discussion groups where the girls discussed their experiences in their school related to being Black females, and during those sessions I often offered up my own stories as a way to contextualize their experiences. As an ally, I offered comments that validated the girls' thinking and assessment of their experiences, and asked pointed questions that helped the girls conceptualize their ideas for activism in their schools. Taken together, the work that I did as a researcher, educator and/or facilitator, and ally all functioned as an intervention on the development of BGCL throughout this study.

The reciprocal nature between my role as a researcher and the BGCL components is evident in how the girls' descriptions and displays of their emotions, their assessment and critiques of their school culture, and the ways they enacted agency, resistance, and self-definition all gave me a window into their worlds. As an outsider, I had a limited understanding of the daily lives of Black adolescent girls who attend independent schools. The knowledge that the girls shared with me caused me to reflect on my own identities and the critical literacies that I hold as a Black woman of a different generation. In a research sense, the girls' actions connected to their BGCL also influenced how I approached the project as a researcher, so that what topic I chose to present in the next girls' group meeting or what follow-up questions I included as part of my interview protocols were in response to what the girls had previously shared.

Conclusion

This chapter presented an emerging theory to understand how Black girls recognize, process, and respond to encounters of race, gender, and class. Situated within the contexts of elite, predominantly white independent schools, the preliminary theory shows how the components of a developing critical consciousness, emotional literacy, and a sense of activism and agency interact with the independent school culture to create a unique set of competencies and strategies that Black girls develop and enact to navigate their school environment while also constructing their sense of self.

From a theoretical perspective, BGCL will contribute to literature focusing on youth racial literacy (Stevenson 2014) and other critical lenses youth employ to understand social and relational interactions in their worlds. Currently, most of the empirical research that examines racial literacy focuses mostly on Black boys or young men (Stevenson 2014). What racial literacy and other literacies look like for Black girls and, in particular, Black girls in independent schools, has yet to be fully studied. To that end, the BGCL theory builds on the framework of Black girlhood (Brown 2013) by examining what sources of agency and competencies come together to create a particular critical lens that Black girls employ in relation to the construction of their adolescent Black female identities, as well as provides a framework through which the experiences of adolescent Black girls can be adequately privileged and contextualized.

From a practice-based and developmental perspective, the presence of sources that foster BGCL when situated in independent schools could contribute to the positive development of adolescent Black girls who attend school in elite, predominantly white settings. Weekly discussion groups, which formed the basis of the BGCL research study, provided a space where adolescent Black girls had the freedom to be critical of institutional systems and spaces and their locations in them, with the goal toward dismantling these structures and working toward the collective empowerment of Black girls and women.

This chapter showed that at the core of this form of BlackGirl-Magic is the development of a critical consciousness where Black girls are able to identify how power operates through interpersonal, intergroup, and societal interactions. This critical consciousness provides Black girls with a foundation for how to be powerful and agentic rather than victims of dominance. Through engaging in multilevel critique, emotional literacy, and activism, Black girls demonstrate their brilliance, their self-definition, their confidence, and their magic as they navigate through their daily lives.

A Black Critical Literacies Study
Introductory Questionnaire Protocol[5]

Thank you for your interest in participating in the Black girl critical literacies study! Please take a moment to complete this introductory questionnaire. Completing this questionnaire is completely optional and you may stop taking the questionnaire at any time. You are free to leave any questions blank that you do not feel comfortable answering. Only the researcher (Charlotte E. Jacobs) will view your responses.

Your name:

Your age:

Your current grade:

1. How would you describe your racial or ethnic background?
2. What broad categories best fit your racial and ethnic background (as described above)? Please select all that apply:

    ____ American Indian   ____ Asian

    ____ Hispanic/Latino   ____ White

    ____ Alaska Native   ____ Black or African

    ____ Native Hawaiian or   American

          Other Pacific Islander

3. How easy is it for you to talk about race?

    ____ Very hard   ____ Easy

    ____ Hard   ____ Very easy

    ____ In the middle

4. How much do you talk with your parents about racism and discrimination against Black people?

    _____ Not at all   _____ A lot

    _____ A little   _____ All of the time

    _____ Somewhat

5. How much do you talk with your friends about racism and discrimination against Black people?

    _____ Not at all   _____ A lot

    _____ A little   _____ All of the time

    _____ Somewhat

6. Have you ever had any experiences of racist acts against you?

    _____ Yes   _____ No

7. If yes, where did this incident occur? Check all that apply.

    _____ My neighborhood   _____ Public places (mall,

    _____ My school   supermarket, park)

    _____ With family/at home

8. In general, how comfortable do you feel responding to racist experiences that you may have?

    _____ Very uncomfortable   _____ Comfortable

    _____ Uncomfortable   _____ Very comfortable

    _____ In the middle

9. How easy is it for you to talk about gender or being a girl/woman?

    _____ Very hard   _____ Easy

    _____ Hard   _____ Very easy

    _____ In the middle

10. How much do you talk with your parents about sexism and discrimination against women and girls?

    _____ Not at all   _____ A lot

    _____ A little   _____ All of the time

    _____ Somewhat

11. How much do you talk with your friends about sexism and discrimination against women and girls?

_____ Not at all   _____ A lot

_____ A little   _____ All of the time

_____ Somewhat

12. Have you ever had any experiences of sexist (discrimination based on being a girl) acts against you?

_____ Yes   _____ No

13. If yes, where did this incident occur? Check all that apply.

_____ My neighborhood   _____ Public places (mall,

_____ My school   supermarket, park)

_____ With family/at home

14. In general, how comfortable do you feel responding to sexist (discrimination based on being a girl) experiences that you may have?

_____ Very uncomfortable   _____ Comfortable

_____ Uncomfortable   _____ Very comfortable

_____ In the middle

15. How easy is it for you to talk about socioeconomic status/class?

_____ Very hard   _____ Easy

_____ Hard   _____ Very easy

_____ In the middle

16. How much do you talk with your parents about classism and discrimination against low-income people?

_____ Not at all   _____ A lot

_____ A little   _____ All of the time

_____ Somewhat

17. How much do you talk with your friends about classism and discrimination against low-income people?

_____ Not at all   _____ A lot

_____ A little   _____ All of the time

_____ Somewhat

18. Have you ever had any experiences of classist (discrimination based on socioeconomic status) acts against you?

_____ Yes   _____ No

19. If yes, where did this incident occur? Check all that apply.

_____ My neighborhood   _____ Public places (mall,
_____ My school   supermarket, park)
_____ With family/at home

20. In general, how comfortable do you feel responding to classist (discrimination based on socioeconomic status) experiences that you may have?

_____ Very uncomfortable   _____ Comfortable
_____ Uncomfortable   _____ Very comfortable
_____ In the middle

School Environment

21. In general, teachers at my school talk about race:

_____ Never   _____ Somewhat frequently
_____ Occasionally   _____ All the time

22. In general, teachers at my school talk about gender:

_____ Never   _____ Somewhat frequently
_____ Occasionally   _____ All the time

23. In general, teachers at my school talk about socioeconomic status/class issues:

_____ Never   _____ Somewhat frequently
_____ Occasionally   _____ All the time

24. I have seen and/or heard stereotypes about Black people at my school:

_____ Never   _____ Somewhat frequently
_____ Occasionally   _____ All the time

25. I have seen and/or heard stereotypes about women and girls at my school:

_____ Never   _____ Somewhat frequently
_____ Occasionally   _____ All the time

26. I have seen and/or heard stereotypes about low-income people at my school:

____ Never   ____ Somewhat frequently

____ Occasionally   ____ All the time

27. How do you define *feminism*?

28. How do you define *oppression*?

29. Do you believe that everyone in the United States has an equal opportunity to be successful?

____ Yes   ____ Unsure   ____ No

Please explain your answer:

30. Is there anything else you would like to share? If so, please write your response here:

Thank you for completing the questionnaire!

Notes

1. In order to maintain confidentiality, all participants and school sites have been given pseudonyms.

2. Independent schools, according to the National Association of Independent Schools, the accrediting body for over 1,400 independent schools in the United States, are "non-profit private schools that are independent in philosophy: each is driven by a unique mission. They are also independent in the way they are managed and financed: each is governed by [an] independent board of trustees and each is primarily supported through tuition payments and charitable contributions. They are accountable to their communities and are accredited by state-approving accrediting bodies" (NAIS 2019).

3. This study was reviewed and approved by the University of Pennsylvania Human Subjects Institutional Review Board in November 2014.

4. The questionnaires protocols were inspired by Howard C. Stevenson, 2012, Parent Information Form, Preventing Long-term Anger and Aggression in Youth (PLAAY) Research Project (University of Pennsylvania, Philadelphia).

5.   These protocols are an abbreviated version of the questionnaires used in the research study. Please contact the author to see the full questionnaire protocols.

Works Cited

Alexander-Snow, Mia. 1999. "Two African American Women Graduates of Historically White Boarding Schools and Their Social Integration at a Traditionally White University." *Journal of Negro Education* 68 (1): 106–19.

Bishop, Anne. 2002. *Becoming an Ally: Breaking the Cycle of Oppression in People.* New York: Zed Books.

Bowles, Samuel, and Herbert Gintis. 1976. *Schooling in Capitalist America: Educational Reform and the Contradictions Of Economic Life.* New York: Basic Books.

Brown, Ruth Nicole. 2013. *Hear our Truths: The Creative Potential of Black Girlhood.* Champaign: University of Illinois Press.

Cary, Lorene. 1991. *Black Ice.* New York: Alfred A. Knopf.

Chase, Sarah. 2008. *Perfectly Prep: Gender Extremes at a New England Prep School.* New York: Oxford University Press.

Collins, Patricia Hill. 1986. "Learning from the Outsider Within: The Sociological Significance of Black Feminist Thought." *Social Problems* 33 (6): S14–S32.

———. 2000. *Black Feminist Thought: Knowledge, Consciousness, and the Politics of Empowerment.* 2nd ed. New York: Routledge.

Corbin, Juliet, and Anselm Strauss. 2015. *Basics of Qualitative Research: Techniques and Procedures for Developing Grounded Theory.* 4th ed. Thousand Oaks, Calif.: SAGE.

Crenshaw, Kimberlé. 1991. "Mapping the Margins: Intersectionality, Identity Politics, and Violence against Women of Color." *Stanford Law Review* 43 (6): 1241–99.

Domhoff, G. William. 2005. *Who Rules America? Power, Politics, and Social Change.* 5th ed. New York: McGraw-Hill.

Evans-Winters, Venus E., and Girls for Gender Equity. 2017. "Flipping the Script: The Dangerous Bodies of Girls of Color." *Cultural Studies↔Critical Methodologies* 17 (5): 415–23.

Evans-Winters, Venus E., and Jennifer Esposito. 2010. "Other People's Daughters: Critical Race Feminism and Black Girls' Education." *Journal of Educational Foundations* 24 (1–2): 11–24.

Freire, Paulo. 2000. *Pedagogy of the Oppressed*. New York: Bloomsbury.

Gaztambide-Fernández, Rubén A. 2009. "What Is an Elite Boarding School?" *Review of Educational Research* 79 (3): 1090–1128.

Gaztambide-Fernández, Rubén A., and Raygine DiAquoi. 2010. "A Part and Apart: Students of Color Negotiating Boundaries at an Elite Boarding School." In *Educating Elites: Class Privilege and Educational Advantage*, edited by Adam Howard and Rubén A. Gaztambide-Fernández, 55–78. Lanham, Md.: Rowman and Littlefield.

Gibson, Gloria A. 2015. "Education vs. Schooling: Black Adolescent Females Fight for an Education in the 21st Century." In *Black Girls and Adolescents: Facing the Challenges*, edited by Catherine Fisher Collins, 199–201. Santa Barbara, Calif.: Praeger.

Goleman, Daniel. 2006. *Emotional Intelligence*. New York: Bantam.

Hill, Shirley A. 2002. "Teaching and Doing Gender in African American Families." *Sex Roles* 47 (11): 493–506.

hooks, bell. 1990. *Yearning: Race, Gender, and Cultural Politics*. Boston, Mass.: South End Press.

hooks, bell. 2014. *Teaching to Transgress*. New York: Routledge.

Horvat, Erin McNamara, and Anthony Lising Antonio. 1999. "'Hey, Those Shoes Are out of Uniform': African American Girls in an Elite High School and the Importance of Habitus." *Anthropology and Education Quarterly* 30 (3): 317–42.

Jones, Jessica J. 2015. "The Mis-education of Black Girls: Learning in a White System." In *Black Girls and Adolescents: Facing the Challenges*, edited by Catherine Fisher Collins, 269–86. Santa Barbara, Calif.: Praeger.

Karabel, Jerome. 2006. *The Chosen: The Hidden History of Admission and Exclusion at Harvard, Yale, and Princeton*. New York: Houghton Mifflin Harcourt.

Loughridge, Mikie, and Loren R. Tarantino. 2004. *Leading Effective Secondary School Reform: Your Guide to Strategies That Work*. Thousand Oaks, Calif.: Corwin Press.

McLaren, Peter. 2015. *Life in Schools: An Introduction to Critical Pedagogy in the Foundations of Education*. New York: Routledge.

Morris, Edward W. 2007. "'Ladies' or 'Loudies'? Perceptions and Experiences of Black Girls in Classrooms." *Youth and Society* 38 (4): 490–515.

National Association of Independent Schools (NAIS). 2016. "Facts at a Glance." https://www.nais.org/media/Nais/Statistics/Documents/FactsAtaGlance AllNAISMembers2018.pdf.

National Association of Independent Schools (NAIS). 2019. "About NAIS." https://www.nais.org/about/about-nais/.

Slaughter, Diana T., and Deborah J. Johnson. 1988. *Visible Now: Blacks in Private Schools*. Contributions in Afro-American and African Studies Number 116. Westport, Conn.: Greenwood Press.

Slaughter-Defoe, Diana T., Howard C. Stevenson, Edith G. Arrington, and Deborah J. Johnson, eds. 2012. *Black Educational Choice: Assessing the Private and Public Alternatives to Traditional K–12 Public Schools*. Santa Barbara, Calif.: Praeger.

Stevenson, Howard C. 2014. *Promoting Racial Literacy in Schools: Differences That Make a Difference*. New York: Teachers College Press.

Sue, Derald W., Christina Capoilupo, Gina Torino, Jennifer Bucceri, Aisha Holder, Kevin Nadal, and Marta Esquilin. 2007. "Racial Microaggressions in Everyday Life: Implications for Clinical Practice." *American Psychologist* 62 (4): 271–86.

Ward, Janie V. 1990. *The Skin We're In: Teaching Our Children to be Emotionally Strong, Socially Smart, Spiritually Connected*. New York: Free Press.

White, Erica S. 2013. *When and Where I Enter: A Study of the Experiences of African-American Girls in All-Girls' Independent Schools*. Shaker Heights, Ohio: Center for Research on Girls at Laurel School. https://www.ncgs.org/wp-content/uploads/2017/11/When-and-Where-I-Enter-A-Study-of-the-Experiences-of-African-American-Girls-in-All-Girls-Independent-Schools.pdf.

CHAPTER 4

WHAT WE KNOW AND HOW WE KNOW IT?

Defining Black Girlhood Spirituality

Porshé R. Garner

Introduction

Following the tradition of Black feminists and womanists, Saving Our Lives Hear Our Truths (SOLHOT), a site of Black girlhood praxis, asks: What do you know and how do you know it?[1] From a Black feminist perspective, this question politicizes our personal experience as being complex, and the place from which we organize and theorize (Amoah 1997; Christian 2000; Collins 2000; Combahee River Collective 2000). From a womanist perspective, this question not only politicizes our personal experience but demonstrates the ways that our personal experience, from which we organize and theorize, is also spiritual (Maparyan 2012; Phillips 2006; Walker 2006; Alexander 2005). *What do you know and how do you know it?* as a premise for SOLHOT allows us to exist within the "and" of the posed question, which creates a blur. The blur that SOLHOT invokes allows us to not only know what we know but to complicate it as well. It is through grappling with the blur invoked by SOLHOT that I am able to see and name Black girlhood spirituality, a conscious acknowledgment of Black girls' relation to the divine and/or invisible realm as sustaining all existence in the material and supernatural worlds. I begin this chapter by unpacking my response to the question *What do you know and how do you know it?* to explain the SOLHOT blur. Next, I map the ideas and concepts brought forth through the blur to conceptualize Black girlhood spirituality. Specifically, this mapping consists of tracing the ways Black feminist, womanist, and Black girlhood scholars are in conversation with SOLHOT to imagine that which comes forth through the blur. I conclude this chapter by providing a definition and example of Black girlhood spirituality.

What Do You Know and How Do You Know It? A Movement Toward the SOLHOT Blur

Sometimes the framing question, *What do you know and how do you know it?*, is taken up by the girls in SOLHOT as: who raised you and what did they teach you?[2] The question, when asked this way, gets directly to the heart of *What you do you know and how do you know it?* I'll unpack my response to this question as an example that gets to the SOLHOT blur. My answer: My paternal grandmother, Lurine Terrell Garner, known to me as Grandma LuLu, raised me, although not exclusively. One of the many lessons she taught me was that education was the key to success and that a strong, spiritual foundation via Christianity would assist and ground me in my pursuit of education. Early on, I understood my grandmother's teaching to mean that successful matriculation through school systems would lead me to earning the necessary degrees that would be a testament to my success and that my spiritual faith would grow by consistently attending and being active in church. Both schooling and church would require discipline, but in the end if I put forth my best effort, I would be rewarded with opened doors that yielded opportunities for which I had yet to dream. Grandma Lulu was right, and my very simple understanding of her teachings revealed more complexity with the opening of each door.

Heeding my grandmother's instruction about education, during my sophomore year of college, I applied and was accepted into the Ronald E. McNair Postbaccalaureate Achievement Program (McNair).[3] I participated in McNair during the summer of 2008, and with the urging of my then-history professor, Jessica Millward, I was introduced to and worked with Ruth Nicole Brown and the collective SOLHOT. SOLHOT is Brown's life work, and she invited me, that summer, to work alongside the collective that dedicated their efforts to being organized by Black girls for the purpose of Black girlhood celebration. Like the good student that I believed I was, I came ready with what I presumed were "good, educational" questions, questions any blooming scholar, who only viewed education as what the classroom could offer, would want to ask about Black girls and Black girlhood to present their scholarship and interests as "serious," or so I thought. Initially, I wanted to know what the effects of hip-hop were on Black girls. I am positive I chose this point of inquiry because I wanted to make some argument about how "bad" such music was for young girls; unsurprisingly, it was the same music I listened to, enjoyed, and still enjoy. As far as I knew, I had been disciplined through schooling to ask this type of question and to think of myself as not being implicated—myself being inside yet outside of the very thing I wanted to study. Brown advised me away from that deficit framing and suggested that I ask more open-ended questions that framed Black girls as knowers, because we are. The door that my grandmother believed I had yet to dream was finally opened.

The true education I did not know I needed until the door was opened was SOLHOT. SOLHOT is how I have come to know Black girlhood as being full of mystery and depth. I describe Black girlhood as full of mystery and depth because there is so much about Black girlhood that goes beyond the superficial assumptions made by dominant society about Black girls and the beliefs about Black girlhood; for example, that Black girlhood relates to biological identity only (Brown 2013). Yet, the surface of Black girlhood can be mysterious and reveal so much. Through my organizing with SOLHOT, I have been trained to go beyond and ignore dominant assumptions while nuancing the mystery revealed through seemingly shallow side-eye glances, giggles, and intimate eye contact. Moreover, as a collective praxis, SOLHOT envisions and enacts revolutionary Black girlhood independent of the permission or freedom of others. This means that Black girls are free and Black girlhood is freedom (Brown 2013, 1), and that Black girls and Black girlhood could never be an additive to how one sees and interprets the world (Owens et al. 2017), which is why during my summer in McNair, I steered away from viewing hip hop as knowing something about Black girls to Black girls knowing something very important about hip-hop. Rather than an additive, Black girlhood is a worldview that is fluid, contradictory, and political, and is not dependent on notions of fixed identities. With Black girlhood as our worldview, in SOLHOT we invest our time, energy, and creativity to claiming, naming, and otherworld making. Our otherworld making is performed, enacted, and created through rituals, artistic engagement, and imagination, and is dependent on our ability to rely on each other and to recall what we already know as being very necessary.

Recalling what we know as being very necessary is important, as it makes visible the genius that is Black girlhood. SOLHOT is not alone in our celebration of the genius that is Black girlhood. Recent conversations such as #BlackGirlMagic have focused on what Black girls know and do, and they have made this visible through the creation of the hashtag. The Twitter hashtag #BlackGirlMagic was created by CaShawn Thompson, who desired to put language to the mysterious beauty and survival of Black women, particularly as it relates to the invisibility of our labor. In an interview with the *Los Angeles Times*, Thompson states that she uses the term *magic* because "it's something people don't always understand. . . . Our accomplishments might seem to come out of thin air because a lot of times, the only people supporting us are other black women" (quoted in Thomas 2015).

Further, writer Julee Wilson adds to Thompson's articulation by stating that BlackGirlMagic "illustrate[s] the awesomeness of Black women that is about celebrating anything we deem particularly dope, inspiring, or mind-blowing about ourselves" (2016). Similar to our work in SOLHOT, hashtags and phrases, such as BlackGirlMagic, make legible what Black girls know, and they push us to think about how we know what we know in relationship to other Black girls and women. In this way, this chapter makes sense of BlackGirlMagic as not being exclusively or specifically about "shiny Black girls" (Jarmon 2013), which is a neoliberal understanding of Black girls and women that further seeks to make us invisible, instead focusing on the community and relationships built and manifested through Black girlhood that make tangible the depths of what we know and how we know it.

The richness of my grandmother's teachings was further revealed through my time spent creating and enacting Black girlhood freedom in community with SOLHOT. With the very clear question *What do you know and how do you know it?*, what I thought I knew up until that point was disentangled. For example, I realized that education was not as linear as I perceived it, nor was it exclusive to an institution such as school. Linear education had taught me that it was my very singular, very solitary self that made my success possible, and that the source of my knowledge was exclusive to what I learned in school. Yet, asking *What do you know and how do you know it?* allowed me to point back to the source of my knowledge. This created a deviation from the linear, which meant what I knew was beyond institution. Importantly, this way of looking to the past demonstrated the ways we are always building from those who taught us and what we've been taught.

Scholar and SOLHOT homegirl Chamara J. Kwakye illuminated a similar inquiry into origins and knowledge production in her book chapter titled "From Vivi with Love: Studying the Great Migration."[4] Using letters written between a focal participant of her research, Vivi, and her grandmother, Nan, Kwakye writes of the ways that Black girls' theorizing and production of knowledge is not only a tool for "personal liberation" (2016, 109), comparable to how I initially thought about Grandma Lulu's instruction, but that education was a key strategy of decolonization and political practice. Similar to my own revelations, Vivi vocalizes that the study of theory and the application of theory began with those who raised her, such as grandparents, aunts and uncles, cousins, and neighbors. My experience and that of Vivi's echoes the work of Barbara Christian who contended in her essay "Race for Theory" that people of color have "always theorized—but in forms quite different from the Western form of abstract logic. . . . Our theorizing is often in narrative forms in the stories we create, in riddles and proverbs, in the play in language, since dynamic rather than fixed ideas seem more to our liking" (2000, 12). Education for people of color has always been beyond the classroom and ultimately relies on the ways that we make sense of what we have always known. For this reason, what we know is always entangled with how we know it.

What you know and how you know it allows you to always point back to the source, but, even more than that, once you are clear about your answer to *What do you know and how do you know it?*, SOLHOT allows you to trouble that which we know by creating a blur between ideologies positioned as polarized ideas. M. Jacqui Alexander and Chandra Talpade Mohanty, in their introduction to *Feminist Genealogies, Colonial Legacies, Democratic Futures*, discuss how our life's work (especially those of us who make and occupy space within the academy) should strive to dismantle divides between ideas that are thought to be polarized. They write that it is necessary to move away from academic and/or activist divides so that we destabilize binaries and the power inherent in those divides so that we can "recall the genealogy of public intellectuals, radical political education movements, and public scholarship that is anchored in cultures of dissent" (1997, 26). Within the context of their article and this quote,

Alexander and Mohanty are pushing us to understand that activism and community-based work will produce knowledge that will help us access a more transnational feminist analysis, one that helps Black girls and women think through the ways that we are affected locally, globally, and regionally by oppressions that are meant to keep us in a colonial frame of thinking and understanding. Alexander and Mohanty's argument dismantles and blurs the academic-activist divide that situates knowledge production within communities, allowing us to see the ways that Black girls and Black girlhood have more to offer beyond polarized ideas.

To further the conversation of blurring, I turn to M. Jacqui Alexander (2005), who argues that for too long we have thought of our experiences as being only secular; however, our experiences are more than secular—they are sacred. Thinking of our knowledge beyond the secular then allows it to be spiritual, which can then be seen as body praxis, and an example of embodied knowledge. Embodied knowledge allows us to remember the ways our bodies are inscribed with that which we know, functioning as a pathway to knowledge that knits together the mind, body, and spirit (Alexander 2005, 298). This embodiment of knowledge serves to make our lives and experience sacred and therefore spiritual.

Cynthia Dillard (2012), in conversation with Alexander, labels this disentanglement and intelligibility of ourselves a spiritual decolonization. Relying on endarkened and Black feminism, Dillard contends that this decolonization happens through "(re)membering" the things we were seduced to forget. (Re)membering then becomes an act of piece-gathering, of collecting and assembling fragments of a larger whole, of creating and innovating identity for African people that includes African Americans seeing ourselves in the gaze of another and not looking away, but instead looking deeper. Decolonizing through (re)membering who we are in relation to one another—in my case, who I am in relation to Grandma LuLu—implicates our and/or my existence as spiritual. Thinking of ourselves in this way allows us to disrupt Western thinking, which disrupts the order of heteropatriarchal, sexist, homophobic, transphobic, xenophobic, and Islamophobic thinking.

Before SOLHOT, I never considered how intimately Grandma Lulu's lessons of education and spirituality were entangled, and the richness that comes from this knowing. Specifically, I am thinking of how I initially thought of Grandma LuLu's teachings as being particular to my mastery of education within the classroom, and also that education and spirituality were disparate. Through the posing of the afore-mentioned questions, SOLHOT, in conversation with Alexander and Mohanty (1997) and Dillard (2012), allowed me to disentangle my very rudimentary views of education by reminding me that the person who raised me was the first theorist I knew, and that the classroom could never assess that knowledge. Further, SOLHOT reminded me that this new education and the process of unlearning that which I once knew was in fact very spiritual. In this way, education and spirituality became entangled. SOLHOT reminded me that while my dominant practice of spirituality was via Christianity, my grandmother engaged in spirituality beyond organized religion through friendships that she cultivated and maintained, or cooking for her family and others, or the gardening she did each summer.

Through the blur that SOLHOT enacts, I am able to see that Grandma LuLu was pushing me toward imagining how my educa-tion was more than what schooling within institutions offered, and how this new way of thinking about school was indeed spiritual. Although attending church was our most obvious practice, the ways that she created community and family with those who were not tied by bloodlines, her care for others, and her care for our physical neigh-borhood were all part of her spiritual practice. These are the ways that Black feminists and womanists have always understood and theorized spirituality. Understanding spirituality as a point of inquiry that goes beyond institutional affiliations is important, and provides an even better context for how I make sense of the way spirituality is enacted within Black girlhood. In the following section, I contextualize how Black feminist, womanist, and Black girlhood studies have made sense of spirituality to demonstrate the ways they are closely tied to creativity and wholeness. This will be key in understanding the final movement of this chapter where I define and explain the key concepts of Black girlhood spirituality.

Spirituality as Creativity Revealed Through Black Girlhood

Spirituality has been defined and taken up by both Black feminist, womanist, and Black girlhood scholars. Black feminist Akasha Gloria Hull defines spirituality as "involv[ing] a conscious relationship with the realm of spirit, with the invisibly permeating, ultimately positive, divine, and evolutionary energies that give rise to and sustain all that exists" (2001, 2). Further, she posits that Black women incorporate, in addition to more traditional religious practices, "new age" practices into their spirituality. These new age practices include the use of tarot cards, chakra work, psychic enhancement, numerology, and Eastern philosophies of cosmic connectedness. Hull argues that it is through the acknowledgement and practice of "new age spirituality" that we learn to love our whole self while considering our relationship to the planet, which in turn helps us inhabit and be inhabited by the universe.

Womanism, at its core, focuses on and theorizes spirituality. This is what separates it from all other critical theories and social-change modalities (Maparyan 2012, 86). Layli Maparyan defines spirituality as "an acknowledged relationship with the divine/transpersonal/cosmic/invisible realm" whereas religion is defined as a culturally organized tradition used for understanding spirit and spirituality (5). For many women, the Black church (traditionally Protestant) and other organized religions such as Islam, have been a starting point or origin for spiritual knowledge and praxis; however, womanists "as spiritual grazers, see spirit or spirituality everywhere and in everything" (88). Most of the time, religious affiliations and places such as the Black church, become locations where people find community, even at the expense of harm and oppression. However, being in community with those who you love, even when harm appears and you must work through that harm, is also spiritual. According to Maparyan, womanist spirituality is eclectic, synthetic, holistic, personal, visionary, and pragmatic. Said differently, womanist spirituality is made up of many parts that are weaved together creatively to create and establish a new whole. Further, it is defined by the person and envisions a reconciling with each other, nature, and spirit; and goes about this reconciliation through moving energy for the purpose of social change.

To spark social change through spirituality, spirituality has to be understood as being creative, which leads to wholeness. It is only through wholeness that we are able to enact social change. In *Soul Talk: The New Spirituality of African American Women* (2001), Hull argues that once Black women begin to use spiritual power as a political force, creativity opens. In "Poetry is Not Luxury," Audre Lorde (2007) states that it is a deep, dark place within women where spirit grows, and the darkness of this place is because it is ancient and hidden. This spirit that is deep, dark, hidden, and ancient brings forth creative power, and true knowledge and action springs from this creativity. Lorde writes,

> For each of us as women, there is a dark place within, where hidden and growing our true spirit rises. . . . These places of possibility within ourselves are dark because they are ancient and hidden; they have survived and grown strong through that darkness. Within these deep places, each one of us holds an incredible reserve of creativity and

power, of unexamined and unrecorded emotion and feeling. The woman's place of power within each of us is neither white nor surface; it is dark, it is ancient, and it is deep. (2007, 37)

Lorde's articulation of spirit as power and creativity within women draws our attention to the generational aspect of spirit while also echoing that the recognition of the interconnection of these qualities is the only way that we can survive our continued erasure and invisibility to create change.

As it relates to "the creative spirit" and its political nature, June Jordan writes that this component of spirit is manifested through love (2016, 11). Love, Jordan writes, is how we make each other's dreams possible while surviving in a world determined to kill us with hatred. Relative to children, Jordan argues that it is them who make this function of love possible. Importantly, it is our loving relationship with children, especially those who are Black and/or female, that allows us to create the social change necessary for our survival.

Toni Cade Bambara's compellingly creative and most complicated work, *The Salt Eaters* (1992), speaks to the risk found in not seeing oneself as spiritual through creativity and our life's work. When we compartmentalize ourselves into different parts, we jeopardize our wellness. *The Salt Eaters* chronicles the healing breakthrough of Velma Harris, facilitated by Minnie Ransom. Velma suffers a mental break because of her refusal to see herself as being spiritual through her activism and creativity. Her breakthrough and return to self were contingent on the ways that she was able to be whole in all of her identities. Bambara, in thinking with Lorde (2007) and Jordan (2016) here, reverberates the ways that we are unable to experience spiritual depth if we do not acknowledge and claim the ways that we are creative.

Speaking to change manifesting through creativity, Layli Maparyan offers the social change modality called "Luxocracy." Luxocracy is described as a creative center and specifically means "rule by Light"

(2012, 3). She argues that Luxocracy allows for us to see what she calls the "Innate Divinity" in ourselves while recognizing the sacredness of ourselves, others, and all created things. Using this as a center from which we organize and live will eventually cause structural governance to be unnecessary. In this way, Luxocracry self-corrects or realigns the universe.

Black Girlhood and Spirituality

The realignment that Maparyan points us to through Luxocracy is made manifest through the centering of Black girlhood. Through the centering and use of Black girlhood as a lens, we see an application of spirituality that changes the way that we conceptualize the world. Writers such as Bambara and Alice Walker use Black girlhood to conjure spirituality to reveal truths that ultimately get us to freedom. Bambara, when asked if she would consider herself a spiritual being, responded that she would not consider the term "spiritual being" to describe her because it is not adequate. Rather, she says that she tries every day to achieve mind-body-spirit as one word. For Bambara, this seems to address some of the things that the spiritual being tends to leave out (quoted in Hull 2001). Many of Bambara's writings include Black girl characters "who carried messages about the strength of being black and female that are as solid as armor," which allowed for Black girls to see themselves in stories and as the hero (quoted in Holmes 2014, xix). The articulation of striving for wholeness is also what she accomplishes through Black girlhood because it is young women, Bambara claims, that do the work of establishing new language to get us to peace and freedom (quoted in Salaam 2007), which is ultimately what wholeness is about.

In her award-winning text *The Color Purple*, Walker (2003) writes that the novel for her is an undoing of religion and a journey back to spirituality. The novel chronicles the life of a teenage Black girl, Celie, who goes through what Walker terms a spiritual transformation of understanding God as a "patriarchal male supremacist," to under-standing God to be everything and everywhere (2003). The purpose of the story then is to show how one journeys from being "spiritu-ally captive" to breaking free and finding the divine within oneself. Through the life of Celie, Walker is able to disentangle spirituality from this mystery figure, which readers see through the use of "Dear God" in many of her written letters, to later entangle spirituality within the community of those who help her break free from domination. Readers see this through Celie's relationship with Shug Avery and Miss Sophia. At this turning point, we see Celie's letters go from being addressed to God, to herself, or her sister Nettie. The purpose of this text supports Walker's early poetic definition of womanism, which locates womanists as "lov[ing] spirit[s]" (2004). I highlight this point because of the way that Black girlhood is not always explicitly in con-versation with spirituality, but also in thinking of the way that wom-anist theologians point us to knowing God as elsewhere.

Womanist theologian Renita Weems connects spirituality directly to Black girls. In *Showing Mary: How Women Can Share Prayers, Wis-dom, and the Blessings of God*, Weems explores the spirituality and spiritual journey of Black girls and women through the story of Mary, the mother of Jesus. According to Weems, because of the location of Nazareth and an understanding of the people who lived there, as well understanding the Bible through a Black woman's lens, Mary was and is a Black girl. Weems gives in-depth context that allows readers to consider spiritual journeys by exploring Mary's secular and spiritual identity, and relationships to others—namely, her cousin Elizabeth. For Weems, what Mary's story beautifully communicates is that for Black girls "spiritual possibilities are never lacking" (2002, 34). Fur-ther, we are held accountable to our spiritual possibilities through friendships, like the one Mary had with Elizabeth.

Friendship is paramount in SOLHOT, and in SOLHOT we know that in order for there to be the change that spirituality pushes us toward, there must be collectivity. Even while spirituality is a personal journey, the journey is done best within community. In order to establish this community, it must first be made. In *Hear Our Truths: The Creative Potential of Black Girlhood* (2013), Brown writes of homegirls' (those of us who labor to make the space of SOLHOT possible) memories of Black girls and Black girlhood as being sacred and connected to our labor. This highlights the ways that we are interconnected, which opens up our accessible spiritual possibilities when we are in community with one another. Further, through this work, Brown demonstrates the intricacies of togetherness. More specifically, our being with one another is not dependent on the physical sharing of space (although this is most desirable), but our being together, even in the metaphysical, is dependent on how we remember that togetherness is made possible through insistence on centering Black girlhood and Black girls through freedom. The possibility that the way in which we are able to access our labor as sacred is through our labor for Black girlhood, which opens the door to survey our sacredness as being directly accessible through Black girlhood.

Black Girlhood Spirituality

Black girlhood spirituality is the conscious acknowledgment of Black girls' relationships to the divine and/or invisible realm as sustaining all existence in the material and supernatural worlds. What I mean by this is that Black girlhood, as a lens, offers a very particular understanding of spirituality and spiritual practices. Black girlhood provides access to spirituality as revealed through creativity and collectivity, which will ultimately allow us to manifest the social change we so desperately need. Society's acknowledgement of Black girlhood's relationship to the divine presumes Black girlhood is holy and omniscient, and is the way through which the divine and/or invisible realm can be experienced. I contend that Black girlhood spirituality allows us to mobilize ideas, to transform circumstance for the purpose of envisioning power differently, and imagines us in the future that we, Black girls, have already created. Said differently, it is through Black girlhood spirituality that Black girls can exist within hegemonic systems and overcome them by imposing the power that exists within. Black girlhood spirituality calls for a radical (re)imagining of Black girlhood that not only speaks to how Black girls survive but also speaks to how humanity's survival is dependent on our reverence of Black girls and Black girlhood. Beyond this articulation, Black girlhood spirituality pushes us to understand how Black girls make sense of the world.

How Black Girlhood Spirituality Shows Up in SOLHOT

In SOLHOT, we show up just as we are, and for me it has always been intriguing to see how we negotiate being in community with one another. Our differences manifest through our beliefs and how we enact those beliefs. SOLHOT is absolutely not about groupthink, but rather it is about how we can all exist and be together while focusing on celebration, and ensuring that we all are free and remain free. This negotiation that we do in SOLHOT is one moment in which I recognize Black girlhood spirituality coming through.

The language that the girls bring with them to SOLHOT is enough to create a new *Merriam-Webster Dictionary*, and usually requires high-level engagement of contextual clues by homegirls just so that we can keep up with the conversation. Other times we just have to flat-out stop and ask what things mean. During a session of SOLHOT, we discussed the latest terms the girls used to describe each other. Sitting in a big circle, what ensued was a conversation about "bhaddie/bhaddies," "goodie/bhaddies," "goodie/goodies," "nasty thottie bhaddies," "thottiannas," "thots," being "thotish," and individuals. The definitions and characteristics that the girls provided demonstrated how others viewed them, and then how they viewed themselves and each other. During this conversation, the wheels were turning in the girls' minds as they went in-between these categories and most times made concessions about the terms if they got too familiar. On a basic level, the terms could be used to describe "good" and "bad" girls, but as we probed more, cases were made that complicated the list. It existed more so in a blur than these separate qualifying and/or quantifying terms.

One person began describing a "bhaddie/bhaddie" as someone who was a girl who did things for attention, and usually wore leggings and crop tops. One of the other participants, Esha,[5] who was also sitting in the circle, interjected and said, "I wear leggings. My momma lets me dress like that. She just says put on jacket." I had already realized that many of the characteristics the girls were describing were present in our very circle, but I remained silent to see how they would make sense of what they were saying and the implications that it had. Esha continued to interject throughout our conversation with questions about what the descriptions meant for her personally, as she was dressed in a way that reflected the terms, and for other girls. With Esha's interjections, there were many concessions brought about by the rest of the girls in the group. Initially, it made me think that the girls were making distinctions about the types of girls that come to SOLHOT. This line of thinking is a trap that got me caught up in distinctions of "good" vs. "bad," but these uses of language and the negotiations made by the participants goes deeper than this.

Black girlhood spirituality is manifested because the girls actively negotiate their everydayness in a way that complicates how we love one another and allows us to be present. The girls seemed unwilling to exclude or target anyone in the room. What I mean by this is that the girls, while getting lost in their descriptions and definitions, did not consider that those with the same characteristics could be present in the room. Despite that, they did not want others present to feel like they were making judgements about them, especially when there were people present who initially believed that "leggings and crop tops" could reveal something about a girl's character. When Esha raised these points, one girl, Valeena, expressed that she was not referring to Esha in her definitions and descriptions; rather, she was talking about girls who were not present—plus, it is not what you wear but how you wear it. It's not that the girls who fit "bad" behaviors do not come to SOLHOT, leaving only the "good" girls, it means that we are always actively thinking about how we defy the status quo in our everyday-ness. Esha was firm in pushing us into the future with her resistance. Just because those terms were used before to mean particular things about girls (or even males as the girls later revealed), Esha challenged these static identities and characteristics, particularly when the girls each wore things that their parents and guardians brought for them.

I would also like to invoke another example that occurred during a somewhat similar conversation that builds on this example. I would like to point out that many of the same girls were present and it happened around a conversation where many of the terms introduced above were again questioned. This time around, the girls explained that terms like "thot" were used by males to insult the girls. Again, we were told that boys could be called this same term; however, it was not an insult to boys. Iyanna responded, "Yeah you can be a thottie boy," to which Dariana responded, with confusion, "But see I don't understand though. I don't understand how dudes gon' call us thots when we going out with a whole bunch of boys but if they go out with a lot of girls what they supposed to be called? Cool. But the stupid thing is that impresses them; that don't offend them. It impresses them when girls call them thots. They be like, 'Yep I sure do get 'em.'" As a group, we questioned what could or would inflict the same embarrassment or harm for the boys, and the girls responded that you had to target their "manhood." Lotus then provided us with her example: "I came up to this one boy and told him I had a slanger. He got mad and said, 'No, you don't,' and I said, 'Yes, I do.'" In that moment, we all laughed and acknowledged how creative Lotus was. She used the term *slanger* in reference to her having a penis.

Black girl terms that Lotus provides is an example of Black girlhood spirituality because through her everydayness, we are pushed further into the future where patriarchy is unsettled. Lotus takes necessary measures to dismantle a symbol of power exclusive to male patriarchy found in the penis, or slanger. Lotus's creativity is unmatched as she demonstrates her Black girl brilliance by moving power to herself through her Black girl slanger. From Lotus's sharing, I believe she really had the young man spinning and wracking his brain to determine the "truth." More than anything, in that moment, Lotus pushed imagination so that even if power returned back to the patriarchy after her conversation with the male student, it was unsettled so that his slanger could never hold the same power. In this way, we're elevated into the future and closer to the divine, in that the divine is freedom and our freedom can only be maintained if we make room for Black girl slangers. It unsettles patriarchy in such a way that it cannot return back to its original state. The unsettling of patriarchy is what is needed to maintain Black girlhood spirituality.

Conclusion

It is through the SOLHOT blur that I am able to make sense of and access Black girlhood spirituality. Black girlhood spirituality allows us to engage Black girlhood, and their experiences teach us how we encounter the divine in our day-to-day experiences. It allows us to see the ways that Black girlhood, in its everydayness, is sacred and holy. Black girlhood spirituality points us to the embodiment of the divine/invisible realm as being linked to our knowledge production, our bodies, and our future. Black girlhood spirituality allows us to reimagine Black girlhood as not exclusive to binaries, but inclusive of all that lies in between. Particularly, we understand Black girls as knowing something particularly complex about their experiences, which allows them to create the terms and conditions of their lives.

Black girlhood spirituality engages BlackGirlMagic, making tangible the knowledge and technologies that Black girls have always utilized. Particularly, Black girlhood spirituality, similar to BlackGirlMagic, is interested in how we make the impossible possible through the intergenerational and communal know-how that we pass down from generation to generation. Further, both Black girlhood spirituality and BlackGirlMagic seek to make sense of the everyday experiences of Black girls, exemplifying Black girls' navigation of the world. In order to execute spirituality and magic, we, Black girls, recognize what we already know because we have learned the best theory from elders who are important to us, such as my Grandma Lulu. Lastly, in order for magic to be sustained, we must do as Black girlhood spirituality instructs us and affirm the lives, experiences, and knowing of Black girls as holy so that we may be carried into the future that Black girls have already created.

Notes

1. Envisioned by Ruth Nicole Brown, SOLHOT operates throughout the United States and abroad as a physical and intentional site of Black girlhood celebration. The physical site commonly runs on a six-week cycle and takes the place of a youth-serving institution, such as a school. The sessions during the six-week cycle happen once a week for two hours after the school day.

2. The term *girl* is used here to describe participants of SOLHOT who tend to be under the age of eighteen.

3. The Ronald E. McNair Postbaccalaureate Achievement Program is a TRiO grant competition funded by the U.S. Department of Education to encourage and support doctoral study for students from diverse and "disadvantaged" backgrounds. For more information visit https://www2.ed.gov/programs/triomcnair/index.html.

4. The term *homegirl* is used to describe a person in SOLHOT who labors to create the space of Black girlhood celebration, and can also be connected to the ways that Barbara Smith uses the term in her anthology *Home Girls: A Black Feminist Anthology* (2000).

5. Names used in this section are pseudonyms to protect the identity of participants.

Works Cited

Alexander, M. Jacqui. 2005. *Pedagogies of Crossing: Meditations of Feminism, Sexual Politics, Memory, and the Sacred.* Durham, N.C.: Duke University Press.

Alexander, M. Jacqui, and Chandra Talpade Mohanty, eds. 1997. *Feminist Genealogies, Colonial Legacies, Democratic Futures.* New York: Routledge.

Amoah, Jewel. 1997. "Narrative: The Road to Black Feminist Theory." *Berkeley Women's Law Journal* 12 (1): 84–102.

Bambara, Toni Cade. 1996. "Education of a Storyteller." In *Deep Sightings and Rescue Missions: Fiction, Essays, and Conversations,* edited by Toni Morrison, 247–55. New York: Vintage Books.

Brown, Ruth Nicole. 2013. *Hear Our Truths: The Creative Potential of Black Girlhood.* Urbana: University of Illinois Press.

Christian, Barbara. 2000. "The Race for Theory." In *The Black Feminist Reader,* edited by Joy James and Tracy Denean Sharpley-Whiting, 11–23. Malden, Mass.: Blackwell.

Collins, Patricia Hill. 2000. *Black Feminist Thought: Knowledge, Consciousness, and the Politics of Empowerment.* 2nd ed. New York: Routledge.

Combahee River Collective. 2000. "A Black Feminist Statement (1977)." In *The Black Feminist Reader,* edited by Joy James and Tracy Denean Sharpley-Whiting, 261–70. Malden, Mass.: Blackwell.

Crenshaw, Kimberlé Williams, Priscilla Ocen, and Jyoti Nanda. 2015. *Black Girls Matter: Pushed Out, Overpoliced, and Underprotected.* New York: Center for Intersectionality and Social Policy.

Dillard, Cynthia. 2012. *Learning to (Re)Member the Things We've Learned to Forget: Endarkened, Feminisms, Spirituality and the Sacred Nature of Research and Teaching.* New York: Peter Lang.

Holmes, Linda Janet. 2014. *A Joyous Revolt: Toni Cade Bambara, Writer and Activist.* Santa Barbara, Calif.: Praeger.

Hull, Akasha Gloria. 2001. *Soul Talk: The New Spirituality of African American Women.* Rochester, Vt.: Inner Traditions International.

Jarmon, Renina. 2013. *Black Girls Are from the Future: Essays on Race, Digital Creativity, and Pop Culture.* Washington, D.C.: Jarmon Media.

Jordan, June. 2016. "The Creative Spirit: Children's Literature." In *Revolutionary Mothering: Love on the Front Lines,* edited by Alexis Pauline Gumbs, China Martens, and Mai'a Williams, 11–18. Toronto: Between the Lines and PM Press.

Kwakye, Chamara. 2016. "From Vivi With Love: Studying the Great Migration." In *The Fluid Boundaries of Suffrage and Jim Crow: Staking Claims in the American Heartland*, edited by Damaris Hill, 105–20. Lanham, Md.: Lexington Books.

Lorde, Audre. 2007. "Poetry Is Not a Luxury." In *Sister Outsider: Essays and Speeches*, edited by Audre Lorde, 36–39. New York: Crown.

Maparyan, Layli. 2012. *The Womanist Idea*. New York: Routledge.

Owens, Tammy, Durell M. Callier, Jessica L. Robinson, and Porshé R. Garner. 2017. "Towards an Interdisciplinary Field of Black Girlhood Studies." *Departures in Critical Qualitative Research* 6 (3): 116–32.

Phillips, Layli. 2006. "Womanism: On its Own." In *The Womanist Reader*, edited by Layli Phillips, xix–lv. New York: Routledge.

Smith, Barbara. 2000. *Home Girls: A Black Feminist Anthology*. New Brunswick: Rutgers University Press.

Salaam, Kalamu ya. 2007. "Searching for the Mother Tongue: An Interview with Toni Cade." In *Savoring the Salt: The Legacy of Toni Cade Bambara*, edited by Linda Janet Holmes and Cheryl A. Wall, 58–69. Philadelphia, Pa.: Temple University Press.

Thomas, Dexter. 2015. "Why Everyone's Saying Black Girls Are Magic" *LA Times*. September 9. http://www.latimes.com/nation/nationnow/la-na-nn-everyones-saying-black-girls-are-magic-20150909-htmlstory.html.

Walker, Alice. 2003. *The Color Purple*. Wilmington, Mass.: Mariner Books.

Walker, Alice. 2004. *In Search of Our Mothers' Garden: Womanist Prose*. New York: Harcourt.

Walker, Alice. 2006. "Coming Apart (1979)." In *The Womanist Reader*, edited by Layli Phillips, 3–11. New York: Routledge.

Weems, Renita J. 2002. *Showing Mary: How Women Can Share Prayers, Wisdom, and the Blessings of God*. West Bloomfield, Mich.: Warner Books.

Wilson, Julee. 2016. "The Meaning of #Blackgirlmagic, and How You Can Get Some of It." *Huffington Post*. January 12. http://www.huffingtonpost.com/entry/what-is-black-girl-magic-video_us_5694dad4e4b086bc1cd517f4.

CHAPTER 5

CONJURING GHOSTS

Black Girlhood Hauntings and Speculative
Performances of Reappearances

Jessica L. Robinson

Introduction

In 2012, Kasandra Perkins of Kansas City, Missouri, was murdered
by her partner, Jovan Belcher. This same year, I entered a doctoral
program at the University of Illinois, the same institution I graduated
two years prior, and was given the assignment to create a final project
reflective of my academic interests. As I prepared my assignment, I
was confronted with the news of Perkins's death and experienced a
visceral response to the brutal incident. Importantly, I came back to
graduate school to organize and write with and about Black girlhood
in this doctoral program and the Saving Our Lives Hear Our Truths
(SOLHOT) collective, and just as I was preparing to make a claim
about what I came back to this place and city to do, I was reminded
of the kind of work SOLHOT had already prepared me for through its
intentional collective practices. The final project for this proseminar
course resulted in a performance entitled "Kasi to her Homegirls,"
which was influenced by previous work done in SOLHOT as a result
of SOLHOT's intentional work with Black girls and the praxis of Black
feminism.

    Envisioned by Ruth Nicole Brown and brought to life by a collec-
tive of Black women and girls in central Illinois in 2006, SOLHOT is

a collective of people who believe Black girlhood is an embodiment and practice of collective worldmaking with Black girls and women as a means of self-articulation within the collective. This worldmaking is only possible through particular practices such as knowing and remembering, listening to Black girls and women, and collective music-making. These practices make up a repertoire of collective Black girlhood praxis. A repertoire, as theorized by performance studies scholar Diana Taylor, functions as a set of performances that, unlike an archive of those cultural memories that would privilege the written text or narrative of those actions, acknowledges that those performances operate as ever-changing and alive instead of a captured memory. In this way, those performances are scenarios operating as "meaning-making paradigms that structure social environments, behaviors, and potential outcomes" (2003, 28). To this degree, knowing and remembering is a scenario (whenever the practice of performance happens), which acknowledges Black girls and women, in particular, as well as the people and things that make the collective possible.

Additionally, knowing and remembering contributes to our (the collective's) understanding of Black girlhood as an organizing construct invested in alternative modes of being; that is, subversion to anti-Blackness and heteropatriarchy, as central to building power through our relationship and accountability to one another. These scenarios within SOLHOT's repertoire, then, "make visible, yet again, what is already there: the ghosts, the images, the stereotypes" with the goal of recalibration of these scenarios to conjure new futures and renewed stories of the past and present (Taylor 2003, 28). This function of SOLHOT can be described by Terrion L. Williamson in her work *Scandalize My Name* (2016) as a Black feminist practice. Williamson makes the connection between Black social life and Black feminist practice as meaningful ways of living that do not require Blackness to be qualified by ideas of citizenship, value, or representation but instead by the everyday life-making and saving practices

Black women and girls participate in. In this way, Williamson, like
SOLHOT, is invested in exploring the ways death and life are entangled for Black people, and the ways that, because of this precarious
situation, Black women and girls participate in Black feminist practices that require resistance (whether intentional or not) to imperial ideas of being alive. For example, Williamson grapples with discourses around violence, teenage pregnancy campaigns, and practices
like wearing weaves or hair straightening to consider ways in which
adherence to the degradation of these practices reinforces white
supremacist standards. Williamson explores Black social life through
interrogating "the terrain of black female experience . . . made legible
by black women's lives and bodies in the making of a sociality that
is firmly rooted in the black imaginary" (2016, 10). In this way, these
practices inform the life-making and saving practices of Black women
and girls in the everyday, "not circumscribed by the conditions of
its possibility but instead enriched and enlarged by the embrace of
the mundane and everyday" (5). This, then, makes the space possible
to remember someone like Kasi Perkins, and guides a practice like
SOLHOT where the objective is not to ask, Why are Black women and
girls treated inhumanely?—a question we already know the answer
to—but rather, How do we/have we create/d the alternative with what
we already know about ourselves and other Black women and girls?

    With focus on the collective's practice of knowing and remember-
ing, this chapter explores performances of this practice as speculative,
which conjures reappearances of people and ideas invoked through
the practice. Specifically, by tracing our knowing and remembering
through Black feminist texts that influence the work of SOLHOT,
as well as performances of knowing and remembering created in
SOLHOT such as that of "Kasi to Her Homegirls," this chapter theorizes Black girlhood hauntings and the speculative reappearances
explored through Black feminist texts and SOLHOT performances
as a collective self-articulation of Black girlhood. It is not simply a

categorization of a time period or visual representation of a *girl*, but is a nonstatic and imaginative mode that honors the experiences, genius, and contribution of Black girls. This theorization of Black girlhood through imaginative modes offers a tangible, collective practice of BlackGirlMagic through Black women and girls organizing together to create new modes of sensing and seeing each other. BlackGirlMagic, a term associated with the "Black Girls are Magic" movement started in 2013 by CaShawn Thompson, has been used in digital spaces as a way to affirm and acknowledge the accomplishments of Black women. Thompson explains her use of *magic* to point to the invisibility of Black women's labor and work. She states, "Our accomplishments might seem to come out of thin air, because a lot of times, the only people supporting us are other black women" (quoted in Thomas 2015). Similarly, SOLHOT depends on Black women and girls being in collective relationship to one another. This interdependence generates an articulation of power recognized as magic that relies on building community where you live, through collective worldmaking with Black women and girls, to imagine political power outside of capitalism. In this way, this paper puts forth Black girlhood hauntings and speculative reappearances as a critique of neoliberal articulations of the future, and as an exploration of articulating the self through collective acts.

Knowing and Remembering as SOLHOT Speculative Art Practice

To further explore knowing and remembering as practiced in SOL-HOT, and thus influential to the process of creating "Kasi to her Homegirls," this section will look at literature from speculative fiction genres, Black feminist literary works, and previous works of SOLHOT. Importantly, the examples of literature illustrated below are in conversation with one another, and in many ways lean into one another as central to the way in which the work functions. For example, adrienne maree brown and Walidah Imarisha, co-editors of *Octavia's Brood: Science Fiction Stories from Social Justice Movements*, note that by "envision[ing] a world without war, without violence, without prisons, without capitalism, we are engaging in an exercise of speculative fiction" (2015, 3). Their work of speculative fiction writing and curating, referred to as "visionary fiction," complements the ways in which Black women writers, such as June Jordan and Toni Morrison, imagined new worlds and reimagined past worlds in their work. Additionally, this aligns their work with SOLHOT's practice of knowing and remembering, in that it envisions conditions we may not currently be living in but keep imagining through organizing and theorizing wants and needs with Black girls.

The work of knowing and remembering as theorized and learned in SOLHOT, is entrenched in the idea that Black girls, and the people and things Black girls love, operate in a fluctuating state of dead and alive. Therefore, when we know and remember Black girls and women, those people can be physically alive, physically deceased, or unborn. This fluctuating state, or social death, is theorized by Lisa Cacho (2012) as the way people deemed deviant are marked as disposable. This disposability allows for the intentional forgetting of persons not protected under, what bell hooks (2004) calls, an "imperialist white-supremacist capitalist heteropatriarchal" order. Cacho's use of "deviance" is linked to Cathy Cohen's (2004) articulation of "deviance" in reference to people not protected by this order because of Blackness, sexuality, and gender. Because of this glaring reality, knowing and remembering in SOLHOT takes this fluidity of life and death not as a dismissal of the violence and brutality caused by these systems of oppression but instead positions this fluidity as a *haunting*; that is, that which is ever present, with the potential for reappearance of the person harmed through conjuring.

Importantly, this idea of haunting points to Avery Gordon's work, in which she thinks of haunting as "an animated state in which a repressed or unresolved social violence is making itself known" (1997, xvi). Gordon's work attempts to describe "those singular yet repetitive instances . . . when the over-and-done-with comes alive, when what's been in your blind spot comes into view" (xvi). In this way, haunting is an experience in which that which is not visible and expected to be invisible—under modern forms of dispossession, repression, and exploitation—is ever present. Therefore, SOLHOT, as an embodiment of speculative practice, envisions haunting as a mode of organizing with and for Black girlhood. SOLHOT embraces those Black girl hauntings as a way to articulate Black girlhood resistance to imperialist ideas of being "alive."

Similarly, Sharon Holland considers Toni Morrison's *Beloved* a pivotal text about this kind of unstable relationship between life and death, and therefore a direct connection to hauntings made by ghosts of a supposed past. Holland writes that *"Beloved* confronts readers with a persistent sense of simultaneity until all fact, all knowledge about slavery, about history begins to exist as in-between, and therefore fragile" (2000, 2). In particular, Holland places Morrison's work in conversation with other Black women scholars to examine the "relative status of Black women and their invisibility and their haunting of the American imagination" (6). This kind of lens toward invisible hauntings not only acknowledges forms of state-sanctioned violence toward Black women and girls but also uses magical realism, a speculative genre, to create a manifestation of that reckoning in the form of a ghost. The ghost of Beloved operates as a reappearance of the invisible. Therefore, these works grapple with the ways in which SOLHOT and the performances practiced within the collective between Black women and girls, through knowing and remembering, use the speculative to consider the relationship between hauntings and speculative reappearances.

Importantly, Alexis Pauline Gumbs's work, *Speculative Poetics: Audre Lorde as Prologue for Queer Black Futurism*, suggests Audre Lorde's 1971 poem "Prologue" "makes possible the political intervention of [the] Black speculative, specifically through the figure of the vampire" (2011, 131). Gumbs contextualizes Lorde's poem through Jewelle Gomez's novel *The Gilda Stories* and Octavia Butler's science fiction novel *Fledging*. Both Gomez and Butler's texts include an epigraph from Lorde's poem, which Gumbs conceptualizes as a haunting. Through highlighting utopia and horror in Lorde's work, as well as positioning Lorde herself as an "undead poetic subject," Gumbs considers this a precursor to later works of Black speculative genres that cite Lorde, specifically through illustrating Black feminist vampire subjectivity as a Black feminist futurist (130). Thus, she is theorizing the role of Black feminist speculative and fantasy genres as the possibility to speculate on spectral meanings of life. Through what she calls *queer intergenerationality*, Gumbs's work is in conversation with the ways SOLHOT imagines speculative performances, specifically knowing and remembering, in that the intergenerational nature of being in relationship through organizing and imagining futures with Black women and girls does not rely on patriarchal notions of time, and thus operates as a means of speculative form.

Additionally, June Jordan's and M. NourbeSe Philip's works function as a guiding light for knowing and remembering within SOLHOT, and are thus pivotal in the development of "Kasi to Her Homegirls." Jordan's 1988 essay "Nobody Mean More to Me Than You and the Future Life of Willie Jordan" explores Black English through Alice Walker's *The Color Purple* and her student Willie Jordan's tensions with duress in South Africa. Importantly, this essay explores the ways in which language operates as a technology of Black invisibility. The essay points to *The Color Purple* as a text about the invisibility of Black women and girls but also as a way to imagine invoking that which is invisible or forgotten. The course Jordan writes about in this piece was entitled "In Search of the Invisible Black Women," and as she writes, she does so with Walker, not simply to cite her but also to conjure *The Color Purple* and make it visible to the understanding of Black women's writing.

Likewise, she writes with Willie Jordan to explore Black English as a kind of speculative art form contingent on grappling with Black rules of language and the in-between status of Black people seen through Jordan's presence of Walker and Willie Jordan within the essay. In this way, Jordan influences knowing and remembering through ways in which creating with invisibility is possible. Likewise, Philip's *Zong!* (2011) manipulates language, using the incompleteness of words to describe a haunting of the in-betweenness of Black life. In this way, Philip's work provides the opportunity to explore other ways of practicing knowing and remembering, which begs for something other than written language. This connects to Diana Taylor's idea of the repertoire, in that these practices, needed to perform particular kinds of memory within our conditions of a present haunted by an ever-present past, require fluidity. This happens in SOLHOT performances of knowing and remembering through speculative art forms, such as altars, to recognize Black girls we want to bring to the space to remember or acknowledge. Fire and water are used to perform rituals of remembrance so that words don't obstruct but rather work in conjunction with other forms of performance to meditate on haunting and transform it into a speculative reappearance of the person, event, or idea of focus.

Importantly, this work of knowing and remembering requires a particular kind of laboring. "Homegirling," the expression used to denote the role of those people who labor and organize the SOLHOT space, requires a particular type of labor that demands manipulation of time and dependence of other people, as well as physical and emotional implementation of the speculative. Ruth Nicole Brown, scholar and visionary of SOLHOT, writes about homegirling as a sacred experience, and therefore entangled in the kinds of haunting and reappearances detailed above. She writes, "Skilled homegirls put into practice the sacred work of making time, understood as a critical means of deregulating normative privileges" (2013, 53). In this way, Brown notes the practice of making time as a mode of playing with the speculative in spite of the hauntings of oppressive conditions that continue to structure Blackness and Black girlhood. Grappling with the presence of Black girlhood hauntings requires homegirls to imagine SOLHOT and their praxis of Black girlhood within the collective. Brown continues: "Homegirls begin to think of their own personal well-being as connected to SOLHOT's sustainability . . . and believe that Black girlhood encompasses them as well, that the celebration of Black girlhood is also a celebration of Black womanhood, equally complex, and that the celebration of personhood is also a celebration of Black girlhood" (53).

This creates a kind of self-articulation of Black girlhood through knowing and remembering, made possible by embracing haunting while collectively working to conjure ghosts through these speculative performances. Additionally, through articulation of the self through the collective, homegirls manifest an engaged expression of power generated with each other for the sake of conjuring other Black girls' and women's genius.

Creation of "Kasi to Her Homegirls" as Speculative Performance

To further explore the ways knowing and remembering operate as a practice of the SOLHOT repertoire, the following section details the creation of "Kasi to Her Homegirls" as a speculative performance entangled with Black girlhood hauntings and reappearances. In 2012, I entered a doctoral program and was asked in the proseminar course to create a final project reflective of my research interests and reason for going to graduate school. I had returned to my alma mater to pursue a doctoral degree because of organizational and personal ties to the community. While at this school during my undergraduate years, I labored with the SOLHOT collective as a homegirl. Once I graduated, I moved and began working with nonprofits due to resistance to staying the city in which I had lived for four years. However, much like the scaredness discussed in the sections above regarding SOLHOT homegirling, I was moved to return back to the community that grew me as a homegirl. My experience with SOLHOT as an undergrad was truly transformational in that my connection to Black girlhood not only influenced my relationships with other Black women and girls but also my relationship to Blackness and feminist consciousness. Brown describes this as an experience multiple homegirls have had by saying, "Homegirls construct their labor as sacred, in much the same way that Black feminist, womanist and activist organizing traditions that are diasporic and transnationally oriented have named labor useful" (2013, 50). My labor with SOLHOT built a kind of connectedness to Black girlhood that insisted on being in community with Black girls as primary and understood moments together, as the kind of praxis that yielded the most rigorous and just kinds of work. Therefore, I returned to my alma mater, community, and physical SOLHOT space to make that labor my work.

When asked to create a final project reflective of my interests, I knew it would be about Black girlhood since I had come to graduate school with that as my work. I, however, was not sure what I would focus on exactly. I previously worked with Black girls in sex education and wrote about Black girls and sexuality, and wanted to continue to focus on that. I was in the middle of working on a project about Black women and girls' sexuality surveillance in online spaces when I heard about the tragic murder of Kasandra Perkins. As I worked in what was at the time our SOLHOT workspace, one of the homegirls said, "Did

you hear about the football player who murdered his baby mama?"
I went to the internet to see if I could find more information on this
and what I found surfaced as a haunting.

The thought of her brutal death tugged on me for days. As the stories surfaced, it became apparent that the news reports were missing
something really important—Kasandra. Jovan Belcher was a member of the Kansas City Chiefs football franchise and his social status seemed to overshadow his actions. As I read the media sources
covering this murder-suicide, the proof of how much (or little) these
sources cared about Perkins's life became apparent. In this moment of
tragedy, Perkins's death became drowned out with details of Belcher's
career, including, for example, how much money he made from his
position as a football player and what type of car he was driving when
he murdered his girlfriend. In the twister of details of his alleged head
injuries and possible redemptive domestic violence charity past, I
wondered: Where is Kasandra? On the day of newsbreak, we saw
much of Belcher—his greatness, his downfall, and his support but
Perkins was seemingly invisible, floating around these stories as a
ghost instead of being the focus. I continued to look for stories about
her and what I found was bittersweet.

Initially, the stories were looking for answers for Perkins's defense.
Questions surfaced such as, "Where was she that night? What made
him upset?" People wanted answers. As I continued to look, I was able
to find her family plea to not let her get overshadowed by who her
murderer was. Importantly, I found popular feminist blogs looking
for Perkins as well. Robin Boylorn of the Crunk Feminist Collective
wrote, "I don't know what caused him to murder Kasandra, but what
I do know is that it was not Kasandra's fault" (2013). This response
revealed the ways in which Belcher's notoriety created protection
dependent on the erasure of Perkins. Lindy West of *Jezebel*, a popular
feminist online media source, also crafted a blog post to highlight the
few comments news outlets mentioned about Perkins's life. In her

quest to keep the name of Perkins alive, she says, "We, the American public, need to examine the fact that our *first instinct*, upon learning of Perkins and Belcher's deaths, was to cast about for any reason that it might *not* be a classic domestic violence narrative. That is a problem. Our priorities, here, are broken" (2012). West's response highlights the need for making sense of the brutality of Perkins and Belcher's fatal relationship stems from a deeper issue, one connected to the fragility of being alive that, for Black women and girls, is exposed when these incidents occur and are documented for the public to consume. In "Sense and Subjectivity," Fiona Ngo explores how "seeing is posited as knowing and yet fails to know; and second, that being seen creates a tension between being known as an object of study and remaining unknown as a subject" (2011, 96). In relationship to Perkins's murder and Black girlhood hauntings, that which is made supposedly visible through media coverage functions as a kind of seeing and not knowing by way of creating a set of documentation surrounding Perkins's murder, giving prominence to that very thing that made the murder possible and what allows for the conditions with which the ghost represents for Perkins's murder. In other words, to simply read about Perkins through media outlets influenced by American public articulations of Black women and girls as a perpetual state of visibility for other folks' consumption and nothing else, also known as servitude, is the kind of problem with the archive Taylor is pushing against, with urgency to create repertoires of performances constructing alternative memories opposite those that collude with white supremacist, heteronormative structures of power.

In this way, the process through which I practiced creating these kinds of alternative memories was through SOLHOT as a homegirl. Through SOLHOT, the practice starts with, What happened to the Black girl? and, What should we do/say/build to acknowledge the ghost and create with it? Brown acknowledges this in connection to knowing and remembering as a practice of Black girlhood by

SOLHOT. She states, "SOLHOT requires creating something that has never quite existed, as we've known it, and in order to do this, rituals of remembering are required" (2013, 47). One example of the way this has been done through homegirling is through the work of *Lovenloops*. A SOLHOT homegirl and sonic artist, *Lovenloops* uses samples of conversations with family (in the invisible and visible world) and memories of home and ideas of Black girlhood as an articulation of freedom to create an album entitled "Don't Ever Forget It." In this way, *Lovenloops* conjures family, memories of life and death, and intimate connections that, under conditions of neoliberal forgetfulness, would deem these things nonexistent. Through this, she uses afro-futurism in the same way Krista Franklin notes in reference to the term to curator, Tempestt Hazel (2012) as "people of color making music and sounds with machines", to create a soundscape insistent on memory and creation as imperative.

Likewise, an ensemble performance entitled *The Rhythm, The Rhyme and The Reason*, co-authored by SOLHOT homegirls Brown, Chamara Kwakye, and Claudine Taaffe (2008), is a performance about the processes of organizing a space such as SOLHOT that relies on Black girlhood as an organizing construct. In this performance, one scene in particular recalls the murder of Sakia Gunn, a queer and/or AG Black girl who was attacked in New Jersey while out with a group of friends. The performer in this scene, Brown, stages the location of Gunn's death through performing as a Black queer and/or AG girl to confront the audience and provide a critique of the conditions that made her murder possible. Media scholar Sarah Projansky notes in regard to this performance that Gunn is present not only as a visual representation by Brown but also "as a queer Black girl who matters to the character in the play, to Brown as a playwright and scholar, and (through engagement with the performance) to the audience" (2014, 179). In this way, Gunn's haunting is conjured through another Black queer and/or AG girl to create an active memory of her. Because of this engagement with Black girlhood haunting through SOLHOT, knowing and remembering was an obligation I took seriously as a part of the sacred work of SOLHOT. When I began to write about Kasandra Perkins these are the words that found me:

I have a memory for everyone to carry.

To remember.

Kasandra Perkins.

Twenty-two.

Kansas City dweller.

Mother.

Daughter.

Dead.

He looked her in her eye and pulled back. 9 times.

Point. Blank . . . Present.

He left.

He called his own life.

Murder-Suicide.

Sunday morning I read the accounts on the web.

*PAGES. Upon. PAGES of standing ovation for the man who coldly
    murdered the mother of his child and then murdered himself.*

Accounts dating back to 2008 of what an awesome man he was.

*How he loved women. How he stood up for them. How he most pub-
    licly loved and praised his mother.*

The woman who raised him.

They said "how could he when he loved women so much"

Apparently not enough.

Justified.

The JUST came from all angles.

"He has abandonment issues from not having a father"

BOOM

"He has injuries from football"

BOOM

"He was an advocate against violence so she must have . . ."

BOOM

"She must have been LOOKING for Trey Songz at that concert"

BOOM

"She must not have been properly taking care of their daughter because
   why would he"

BOOM

"She was a young woman with a football player, must've been a gold
   digger and he just couldn't"

BOOM

BOOM

BOOM

"Couldn't handle her"

BOOM

Faded away.

Missed the headline.

SHE

is Kasandra Perkins and she can only exist in our memories.

SHE

was a young woman who went to a concert with a friend and the next
   morning became a shadow of her murderer.

SHE

became a target for every name, emotion, and idea that this society can
   create, manipulate, and say about young Black women who have
   children with rich men.

Would we rather wish that Kasi was out in the club with her girlfriends
   looking for Trey Songz?

That she "trapped" him for his money?

That he was so mentally unstable that her life doesn't matter anymore?

That his life is more important?

That we cannot even name her as Kasandra but only as Jovan's girl-
  friend or the more useful—baby mama?
do we wish that these things are true so that we can make sense of it,
  feel comfortable in our current discourse around?
women.
love.
practice.
baby having/keeping/making . . .
9
Times.
Point.
Blank.
Present.
Brought about several articles, responses, and critiques of how she was
  justifiably murdered.
Murdered and forgotten
I want you all to know and remember Kasandra Perkins
Kasi to her homegirls.
I will always remember her and everything that her story teaches us
  about representation, love, and fear.
dear god I wonder can you save me because I wish to live.
Point. Blank. Present.
Remembered.

As stated earlier, in conversation with Jordan's and Philip's articulations of the limits of language, these words, a response to how I
felt about Perkins's murder, guide a verbal and sounded performance
that moves knowing and remembering to an embodied experience,
which allows for not just what is seen to be knowledge but what is felt
and heard to be knowledge as well.

I was nervous to present this work, which had been created based
on an actual Black girl death but also encouraged SOLHOT's insistence

on knowing and remembering Black girls and women. I was, after
all, not presenting to my homegirls but to my colleagues, who did
not necessarily understand the work our collective did or accept it
as academically rigorous or artistic because of the constraints of disciplinary constructions, and expectations that final work be written
in a standard twenty-page paper format. However, the first response
I received from my colleagues proved that the conjure was indeed
present. Following the performance, they asked: Did you know her?
Is she your friend? For me, a scholar practicing Black girlhood as a
collective mode of being connected to, listening to, believing, and
being in community with Black girls and women while building relationships, power, and articulations of who we are through our time
together and in connection to one another, the acknowledgment of a
"friend" meant that Perkins and the alternative memory, told through
the SOLHOT practice of her tragic murder, had speculatively shown
up in that room. In this way, knowing and remembering operates as
a way of recasting hauntings into speculative reappearances of Black
girls gone too soon; not simply as a way to tell a story but to reconfigure the memory as an ever-present acknowledgment of Black girlhood through conjuring.

Black Girlhood Through SOLHOT and
Self-Articulation Through Collective Practices

In *Feminist Genealogies, Colonial Legacies, Democratic Futures*,
M. Jacqui Alexander and Chandra Talpade Mohanty ask: "What
kinds of transformative practices are needed in order to develop
non-hegemonic selves?" (1997, xxvi). In this way, I imagine Black
girlhood, as theorized through Black feminist genealogies practiced
through SOLHOT, as a praxis of transformation. It is a way of seeing

that requires emotional and physical labor as articulated through SOLHOT practices, which call for collectivity, imagining artistic and intellectual resources as one in the same, and positions relationships and organizing with Black girls as primary to the work. This process of imagining Black girlhood in community with one another is a process of decolonization prompted by Alexander and Mohanty. Alexander and Mohanty imagine decolonization as "thinking of oneself out of the spaces of domination, but always *within* the context of collective and communal process . . . which happens only through action and reflection, through praxis" (xxvii). I imagine SOLHOT's work, and thus the work of knowing and remembering Black girlhood through Black girls, done through speculative performances. One of the ways this is possible is through feminist organizing. Imagining oneself (and the collective, per Alexander and Mohanty's instruction) out- side of domination puts Black feminist futurity into practice, creating a praxis of Black girlhood that relies on imagining Black girlhood through speculative forms to honor our connections to those Black girls gone too soon. It guides our organizing as ancestors, as well as Black girls (in their complexity), currently physically living.

Thinking with speculative forms allows activists, artists, and scholars to critique the conditions that concepts of modernity rely on. Scholars have long considered the connections between current global polit- ical and social conditions and the lasting impact of imperialism and colonialism. When these connections are considered, what becomes present are the hauntings of imperialism and colonialism, and thus capitalism, as a tension against a radical Black girlhood that critiques a commodified version of itself, where participation and interest require the buying and selling of Black girlhood as culture. Rethink- ing this process by conceptualizing Black girlhood practices through speculative forms offers a different possibility for what the exchange of resources not reliant on capital gain might offer.

Additionally, creating with speculative forms allows an opportunity to engage the communal practice of remembering to articulate the self. Brown states, "To homegirl is to commit to a very sincere practice of remembering Black girlhood as a way to honor oneself and to practice the selflessness necessary to honor someone else, remembered whole" (2013, 47). Brown's call for a practice of selflessness that enables homegirls to remember someone else whole is a practice of pushing back against neoliberal demands for individuality and self-reliance. Therefore, the practice of remembering others, as explored in "Kasi to Her Homegirls" and other SOLHOT knowing and remembering performances, imagines the self in community and thus refuses neoliberal demands. It creates a performance of power recognized as magic that centers practices of Black girls' and women's work together as the powerful force that does the political work of imagining and enacting what freedom might feel like for Black women and girls.

Influenced by multiple fields, this work contributes to Black girlhood studies by centering the experiences and lives of people socialized through Black girlhood. It also imagines the political possibilities of organizing with Black girlhood that is not solely dependent on identity politics, but also not void of them. Moreover, this contributes to speculative arts and Black feminism by continuing the work of acknowledging Black girls' genius and creativity as critical to imagining a future.

Works Cited

Alexander, M. Jacqui, and Chandra Talpade Mohanty, eds. 1997. *Feminist Genealogies, Colonial Legacies, Democratic Futures*. New York: Routledge.

Boylorn, Robin. 2012. "Remember Their Names: In Memory of Kasandra, Cherika & Others." *Crunk Feminist Collective*. December 3. https://crunk feministcollective.wordpress.com/2012/12/03/remember-their-names-in -memory-of-kasandra-cherica-others/.

brown, adrienne maree, and Walidah Imarisha, eds. 2015. *Octavia's Brood: Science Fiction Stories from Social Justice Movements*. Chico, Calif.: AK Press.

Brown, Ruth Nicole. 2013. *Hear Our Truths: The Creative Potential of Black Girlhood*. Urbana: University of Illinois Press.

Brown, Ruth Nicole, Chamara Kwakye, and Claudine Taaffe. 2008. *The Rhythm, The Rhyme and The Reason*. Performance. University of Illinois, Krannert Center for Performing Arts, Urbana, September.

Cacho, Lisa M. 2012. *Social Death: Racialized Rightlessness and the Criminalization of the Unprotected*. New York: New York University Press.

Cohen, Cathy. 2004. "Deviance as Resistance: A New Research Agenda for the Study of Black Politics." *Du Bois Review* 1 (1): 27–45.

Gordon, Avery. 1997. *Ghostly Matters: Haunting and the Sociological Imagination*. Minneapolis: University of Minnesota Press.

Gumbs, Alexis Pauline. 2011. "Speculative Poetics: Audre Lorde as Prologue for Queer Black Futurism." In *The Black Imagination, Science Fiction, Futurism and the Speculative*, edited by Sandra Jackson and Julie E. Moody-Freeman, 130–145. New York: Peter Lang.

Hazel, Tempestt. 2012. "Black to the Future Series: An Interview with Krista Franklin." *Sixty Inches from Center*. May 28. http://sixtyinchesfromcenter .org/archive/?p=15558.

Holland, Sharon. 2000. *Raising the Dead: Readings of Death and (Black) Subjectivity*. Durham, N.C.: Duke University Press.

hooks, bell. 2004. *The Will to Change: Men, Masculinity, and Love*. New York: Simon and Schuster.

Jordan, June. 1988. "Nobody Mean More to Me Than You and the Future Life of Willie Jordan." *Harvard Educational Review* 58 (3): 363–74.

Ngo, Fiona. 2011. "Sense and Subjectivity." *Camera Obscura* 26 (1): 95–128.

Philip, M. NourbeSe. 2011. *Zong!* Middletown, Conn.: Wesleyan University Press.

Projansky, Sarah. 2014. *Spectacular Girls: Media Fascination and Celebrity Culture*. New York: New York University Press.

Taylor, Diana. 2003. *The Archive and the Repertoire: Performing Cultural Memory in the Americas*. Durham, N.C.: Duke University Press.

Thomas, Dexter. 2015. "Why Everyone's Saying Black Girls Are Magic." *LA Times*. September 9. http://www.latimes.com/nation/nationnow/la-na-nn -everyones-saying-black-girls-are-magic-20150909-htmlstory.html.

West, Lindy. 2012. "Let's Talk about Kasandra Perkins for a Change." *Jezebel.*
    December 7. http://jezebel.com/5966425/lets-talk-about-kasandra-perkins
    -for-a-change.
Williamson, Terrion L. 2016. *Scandalize My Name: Black Feminist Practice
    and the Making of Black Social Life.* New York: Fordham University Press.

CHAPTER 6

WHAT DOES #BLACKGIRLMAGIC LOOK LIKE?

The Aesthetics of Black Women's Afropunk Citizenship

Marlo D. David

In 2003, Brooklyn-based musician Tamar-Kali Brown appeared in James Spooner's watershed documentary *Afro-Punk*, which featured interviews with dozens of Black punk performers and fans (Spooner 2003). She is introduced in the film at age twenty-eight, and in her first scene she is seen shaving her head while in voice-over she describes seeing a lot of people of color "in the hardcore scene" while "growing up in the hood." Listening to punk bands, including the Untouchables and Fishbone, she goes on to name Nina Simone as her prototypical "punk angst person." While she narrates, viewers watch Brown dress and, in a side profile image, her shaved head and multiple piercings strike a fierce pose. Her short, kinky, and textured hair begins nearly in the back of her head, leaving just a small circle of hair on her otherwise bald pate. After layering on a hat and hoodies, she is seen throwing two guitars over her shoulder. Later, she describes her affinity for punk as an extension of her Blackness: "Punk rock is Black music," and she explains that the punk aesthetic is what drew her into the genre.

In her second segment of the film, she is seen wearing an African print head wrap as she boards a bus and goes to an apartment. These scenes are cut with images depicting close-ups of her adorned body: a tattoo between her breasts, multiple beaded bracelets, and several facial piercings. She says, "I'm aware of the direct influence of African peoples and Indigenous peoples of America influence on the punk prototype. In hindsight, I understand how it drew me in." She describes being attracted to images of "tribal people," and that she found those images "striking," as the camera lingers over books depicting African people with piercings, dreadlocks, intricate hair braiding, and scarification. Brown admits that the punk adaptations that she adopted—brightly colored hair or safety pin piercings—are often read as "white." Yet, she connects her punk aesthetics to African adornment practices, and in doing so she finds an affinity with an imagined cultural home that exists both in sync with the Black community within her Brooklyn neighborhood and outside of it. Even when faced with accusations of "acting white," Brown explains, "I know exactly who I am being. I have no fear around it. I am very clear."

Brown's comments in the *Afro-Punk* documentary, like many other interviews included in the film, point out how critical personal styling, embodiment, and Blackness are in the process of generating a sense of belonging for those who identify as Afropunk. Cultural critic Greg Tate describes Afropunk artists as "nigras from outer space," and the Afropunk website, afropunk.com, once identified itself as "the other black experience," a phrase that disrupts not only the post-racial myth of the millennial era but also the rhetoric of a singular Black authenticity (Tate 2011). Pushing identity fluidity while remaining unapologetically Black, Afropunk as a cultural movement rejects ideologies of colorblindness that have become the hegemonic response to questions of race in America and other liberal democracies around the world. Once simply a moniker for Black people who participate in hardcore punk scenes, Afropunk has morphed into a wider brand to identify sites of fluidity and transgression, self-expression, and creative exploration that continue to challenge the boundaries of Blackness as a singular "safe space" for all Black people. The documentary, the series of global music and arts festivals, the website, and social media venues collectively produce an identifiable marker of millennial Blackness that is funky, edgy, artsy, quirky, queer, kitschy, and futuristic.

With these conditions in mind, this chapter traces the ways that embodied aesthetics are used by Black women and femmes who participate in the global Afropunk movement to negotiate sites of belonging and collective identification through the production of new Black femininities. Personal styling—hair, fashion, makeup, and body modification such as tattoos, piercings, and contact lenses—allow Afropunk participants to stage critical interventions into the visual vocabulary of contemporary Black womanhood, much in the way that Brown describes her adoption of a punk aesthetic. These are the Black women and girls who style themselves in ways that seem futuristic or retro, too butch, too femme, embellished, excessive, "doing the most," "out there," or weird. They also turn toward African-inspired adornment practices that span the diaspora, from the use of Ankara fabric to the beaded jewelry of southern and eastern Africa. Black women's style historian Tanisha Ford explains that Black women have "turn[ed] getting dressed into a political strategy of visibility" (2015, 4). While Ford's book *Liberated Threads: Black Women, Style, and the Global Politics of Soul* focuses on the circulation of Black women's "soul" style during the Black freedom movements of the mid-twentieth century, this chapter posits Afropunk aesthetics as a contemporary "strategy of visibility" for the millennial era as Black women struggle in the shadow of neoliberalism, postracialism, and the age of the internet. Moreover, I consider Afropunk aesthetics an exemplar of #BlackGirlMagic, thus linking questions of embodiment and materiality to emerging scholarship on Blackness and digital media.

Before CaShawn Thompson used the phrase "Black Girls are Magic" in 2013 as a way to celebrate the achievements of Black women and girls, blogger and cultural critic Renina Jarmon coined the expression "Black Girls Are from the Future" in 2010, and both slogans have become popular hashtags. Thompson said she began using the phrase online "to speak about the positive achievements of black women," while Jarmon describes her concept as a "brand, a narrative, and an oppositional standpoint" adopted by everyday Black women and girls to contend with the multiple marginalizations of race, gender, class, and sexuality. In a 2017 *Nylon* interview, Jarmon traced a genealogy of terms that highlight similar themes, from #QuirkyBlackGirls, a collective of writers started by Alexis Pauline Gumbs and Moya Bailey in 2008, to Zeba Blay's #CareFreeBlackGirl. While these are each examples of what Tara L. Conley describes as "black feminist hashtags," the specific terms in Jarmon's genealogy illustrate alternative conceptions of millennial Black womanhood that centralize achievement, pleasure, self-care, and visibility, along with modes of collectivity that privilege digital community building that can eventually lead to connections in real life (IRL) (Conley 2017). Therefore, within the broad category of the "black feminist hashtag," a subgenre emerges that I call *affirmation codes*. Unlike other Black feminist hashtags, such as #SayHerName or #YouOKSis, that concentrate on naming and identifying specific struggles against state-sanctioned violence faced by Black women and femmes, affirmation codes emphasize optimism, self-definition, media visibility, creativity, and wellness as sources of resistance. Affirmation codes, including their most popular iteration, #BlackGirlMagic, are mobilized primarily as social media hashtags, but they also appear on T-shirts, posters, coffee mugs, and other material objects. Drawing on recent scholarship in Black code studies, the naming of affirmation codes works to center "black thought and cultural production across a range of digital platforms, but especially in social media, where black freedom struggles intersect with black play and death in polymorphic and polyphonic intimacy" (Johnson and Neal 2017, 1).

The ways that affirmation codes turn toward notions of quirkiness, magic, futurism, and freedom cast Black femininity as ethereal or enchanted, but Black womanhood has long been represented through tropes of miracles, conjuring, spirituality, and ancestral presences. Writers such as Audre Lorde, Octavia Butler, Toni Cade Bambara, Toni Morrison, and Ntozakhe Shange have drawn on "magic" to illuminate the joys and pains of Black women's lives. However, this presumption of "otherworldliness" attached to #BlackGirlMagic lends to its mystification and controversies about how affirmation codes should be used, who should use them, and why. For instance, #Black-GirlMagic has been critiqued as a phrase that overlooks the material realities of everyday physical and epistemic violence, and reinforces the controlling images of the "strong Black woman" or the "magical Negro" (Chavers 2016). Further, as affirmation codes have become popular merchandising tools for corporate media franchises and for material goods marketed toward Black women, disputes have arisen about the origins of the phrases and who gets to profit from their use (Hope 2017). There is also the question, posed by the editors of this volume: How does #BlackGirlMagic translate outside of social media? This question attends to the need for Black women's studies scholars to define, analyze, and critique the cultural zeitgeist that these statements represent. While these affirmation codes have become ubiquitous in contemporary Black popular culture, little is known yet about how they function as artifacts of millennial Black life.

Similarly, the *Afro-Punk* documentary and its global music festivals and online presence act as concomitant artifacts of Black life, drawing together alternate visions of Blackness among people who identify in some way with the experiences originally described in the film. Therefore, the Afropunk movement becomes a space to discover how #BlackGirlMagic and other existing or emergent affirmation codes indexed by its naming serve as beacons of belonging in the millennial era. Specifically, I look to the ways that Black women and femmes who perform and participate in Afropunk use their aesthetic choices to mark and hail others into a space of cultural citizenship in ways that function as visual affirmation codes. How have beauty, fashion, and style operated as counterhegemonic texts for unapologetic Black womanhood that often exists at the margins of respectable community acceptance? The affirmation code of Afropunk aesthetics works materially in ways that allow us to theorize what #BlackGirlMagic looks like, and begins to consider its contours on and offline. Further, by engaging in close reading and media analysis of Afropunk fashion coverage in online magazines and blogs, I discuss what happens when these visual affirmation codes are hacked by corporate interests and read by those outside of a space of cultural citizenship.

Afropunk Citizenship

Afropunk citizenship exists as a constellation of Afro-diasporic subjectivities that identify as punk, not the narrowly defined genre of music and style that is conjured by images of white bands like the Sex Pistols or the Clash but the IDGAF attitude of Black postmodernity. It's Trey Ellis's "New Black Aesthetic" 2.0, an intentionally hybrid, genre-defying, queer, code-switching individualism in search of modes of belonging outside of mainstream representations of Black identity (Ellis 1989). Afropunk citizenship has been made widely visible and legible through the production of the documentary and the advent of the first Afropunk fest in Brooklyn in 2005, when fans of the film sought each other via online message boards to gather and party together. Following those successes, Afropunk citizenship has become both *marked* and *generated* by corporate-sponsored global festivals, which include multiple music genres, as well as the website afropunk.com and its social-media presence on Instagram, Twitter, Snapchat, Tumblr, and Facebook. The commingling of personal interaction—at concerts, film screenings, community events, parties, and the like—and digital community building makes this particular form of "cultural citizenship" categorically millennial.

The evolution of Afropunk during the past fifteen years into its current brand has alienated some of the people who originally found a home in its naming, including filmmaker James Spooner, who no longer associates with Afropunk (Kameir 2015). Critics argue that the festival has been gentrified by catering to a growing number of white attendees, engaging in transphobic practices, and trading its countercultural spirit for deals with Mountain Dew, Red Bull, and Doc Martens (Dr. Martens), to name a few of its corporate sponsors (Cepeda 2017; Josephs 2015; Fields 2016; Donnley 2018). Tickets for the weekend of concerts cost seventy-five dollars or more, when they were once free. Platinum-selling rock or R & B headliners like Lenny Kravitz or D'Angelo get top billing over underground, hardcore bands. These critiques have led to a boycott of the festival in recent years, and former fans accuse organizers of erasing the Black punk roots of the event. Nevertheless, Afropunk is more than the festival, and it remains critically relevant to the affirmational, aspirational Black subjectivities of the post-civil rights era, even as its existence begs the question: How can something be punk and "bougie" at the same time?

Theories of Black cultural citizenship offer an approach to this paradox by addressing the function of state power on Black individuals and communities across multiple categories of difference, including class, gender, sexuality, ability, nation, or language. For anthropologist Kamari M. Clarke (2013), Black Atlantic cultural citizenship is constituted by mobile, flexible modes of belonging that operate both beyond and bound to state power. Her work describes how notions of cultural citizenship help us think through the "limits, possibilities, and alternate cartographies of belonging," (Clarke 2013, 466) and when it is taken up in African diasporic contexts, like Afropunk, it necessitates attention to race in the negotiation of memberships and exclusions as well as the "play of politics." In other words, a sense of common racial identity or even geographic proximity is not sufficient for forming the bonds of cultural citizenship. A sense of shared political interests plays an integral part in how members negotiate belonging as well as how they identify their group identity as distinct from juridical or national structures of citizenship. Christen Smith locates this attention to racialization and politics specifically through the "diasporic realities of anti-black state violence" (2015, 366), wherein Black subjects around the world find themselves bound to sites of state violence via the necropolitics of police surveillance and brutality, judicial discrimination, and extralegal killings, among other forms of physical and epistemic violence sanctioned by the state (Smith 2015; Mbembé and Meintjes 2003).

Sites of violence illustrate the incongruities of Black belonging within nation states, because "black people have been disenfranchised (from voting and political participation in particular) but also that they have been symbolically erased as subjects who have even the potential for national belonging" (Smith 2015). As an activist-scholar, Smith has worked in Salvador de Bahia, Brazil, in organizations fighting police brutality, and she reflects upon the fact that "regardless of my geographic location, at home in the United States or abroad in Brazil, the realities of anti-Black state violence followed and engulfed me" (2015, 385). Therefore, Smith studies forms of belonging that exist "far beyond national boundaries . . . [that] include the affectual economies that produce ourselves as racialized, political subjects" (386). Clarke and Smith both emphasize a deliberate reckoning with white supremacy and anti-Black state violence as essential to contemporary forms of global Black consciousness that critique systemic and institutional roots of oppression. This critical posture is what keeps Afropunk "punk." Afropunk citizenship exists at this nexus in which affirmational, aspirational Black attitudes and aesthetics come out to play in the face of the ever-present necropolitics of Black death. Matthew Morgan, who produced the first Afropunk festivals with James Spooner and continues to helm the festival along with business partner Jocelyn Cooper, has been responsible for developing the

contemporary festivals and websites in ways that I see as both marking and generating a sense of belonging for those who seek out the
Afropunk scene. This is how Morgan describes his vision:

> It's the new adoration of all things African. The continent of Africa has
> a humongous part to play in global black consciousness. We're also
> able to communicate online. So the gatekeepers of distribution are no
> longer standing in our way. Young black kids globally want to feel—
> need to feel—good [about themselves], and we are unapologetically
> black, not to the detriment of anyone else. We're seeing images that
> are so destructive to our souls. We're basically watching snuff films
> online on a daily basis. The images are so egregious at times. So putting
> positive images of self and creating an environment where people feel
> truly comfortable and uplifted sounds simple, but it's what we've been
> able to achieve, and it means so much to people. (Fields 2016)

Morgan's articulation of Afropunk citizenship does not hinge solely
on an explicit identification with punk music, skateboarding, or other
countercultures. Instead, he points to the way in which the festival
provides a global alternative to the near-constant scenes of brutality and murder that circulate in media, which he calls "snuff films."
Morgan suggests that pleasure in "unapologetic blackness" acts as a
balm for these "egregious" and "destructive" images, including dash-
board and body camera footage from police stops or videos of violence
filmed by strangers, or even by the victims themselves. Therefore,
Afropunk exists as a method through which diasporic Black cultures
can build community created out of aesthetic longing that functions
as resistance to transnational iterations of anti-Black racism, which
appear in neoliberal, neocolonial, and imperialist forms.

However, any theory of Afropunk citizenship must also take into
account how being *both bound by and beyond state power* is gendered.
If one critical loci of Black cultural citizenship is the ubiquity of global

anti-Black violence, then it is necessary to engage the gendered nature of that injustice because "the unique ways in which Black women and girls experience violent victimization requires unpacking both the gendered dynamics of racial injustice and the racial dynamics of gender injustice" (Lindsey 2018, 163). Efforts such as #SayHerName, #BringBackOurGirls, or the Movement for Black Lives (M4BL) have insisted that the analysis of anti-Black violence include the presence of Black women, femmes, and girls. The masculinization of popular discourse around state-sanctioned violence has rendered trans and cis women invisible (*only Black boys and men are victimized*) or less central to the identification of the problem and strategies of resistance (*Black men must provide analysis and be leaders of the movement*). In response, many activists and scholars have fought for an intersectional approach to understanding how state power is gendered. Historian Marcia Chatelain explains that

> even if women are not the majority of the victims of homicide, the way they are profiled and targeted by police is incredibly gendered. There are now renewed conversations about how sexual violence and sexual intimidation are part of how black women experience racist policing. You don't have to dig deep to see how police brutality is a women's issue—whether it's the terrifying way that Oklahoma City police officer Daniel Holtzclaw preyed on black women in low-income sections of the city, or the murder of seven-year-old Aiyana Stanley-Jones inside her Detroit home. We know that girls and women of color are also dying. (Chatelain and Asoka 2015)

From its outset, the #BlackLivesMatter movement, created by Black queer women—Opal Tometti, Patrice Cullors, and Alicia Garza— emphasized an intersectional approach to addressing multiple forms of racial injustice. However, even their names were originally elided from the popular discourse about their activism. Therefore, as Chatelain notes, it becomes even more imperative to insist that "Black Lives Matter" does "not only mean men's lives or cisgender lives or respectable lives or the lives that are legitimated by state power or privilege" (Chatelain and Asoka 2015). In the wake of these brutal realities, Conley's theorizing of Black women's digital activism becomes even more essential because Black feminist hashtags "represent[s] code. It is a mapping through the noise" (2017, 29) in order to name and resist harm and erasure, and to build solidarity and counter-discourse. Further, Black feminist hashtags "do things. They proliferate to mediate connections across time and space" (Conley 2017, 23). Therefore, I argue that Black women approach Afropunk as "counterpublic networks of crowdsourcing, storytelling, and reporting" (Conley 2017, 24) by centralizing their style and appearance. Black women's Afropunk citizenship inscribes an aesthetic code, an embodied code, an affirmation code, that acts as that "political strategy of visibility" described in Tanisha Ford's (2015) research. Recall the images of Tamar-Kali Brown in the *Afro-Punk* documentary that opened this chapter. Her introduction in the film emphasizes her sartorial practice and serves as a reminder, especially for those who might critique superficiality in contemporary Afropunk cultural production, that punk is always already a "look."

Black Women, Afropunk, and the Street Style Image

In the section that follows, I identify specific aesthetic themes that have been adopted as signifiers of Black women's Afropunk citizenship as they have existed in digital spaces since 2014. I provide a critical visual analysis of images that have been selected after viewing several hundred relevant pictures, examining the images, the accompanying text, and their context in order to understand how Black women viewers make meaning in digital spaces. The primary aesthetic theme examined is *Hairstyle*. Other themes that are present, but will not be explored in this chapter are *Body Modification, Futurism, Florals*, and *Toplessness.* The *Hairstyle* theme addresses the multiple ways that Black women style their hair, including, but not limited to, length, color, texture, size, and the use of extensions and embellishments such as wigs, hairpieces, barrettes, and other stylistic elements. Attention to Black women's "hair politics" has experienced a renewed energy in the millennial era, as conversation about hair styling has moved to the internet. Globally, Black women now have the opportunity to share their experiences styling their uniquely textured hair on blogs and vlogs, revealing their creative techniques and emphasizing DIY methods.

In order to trace this theme, I conducted close readings of online "street style" photo articles about the Brooklyn Afropunk Fest appearing in three prominent mainstream women's fashion publications— *Vogue, Elle*, and *Allure*—as well as *Vogue* coverage of the first Afropunk festival in Johannesburg in January 2018. The photos in these publications help shape some of the prevailing aesthetics of Black women's Afropunk citizenship in part because these images are often the same ones that get pinned on Afropunk-themed Pinterest pages. For the most part, these photo articles appear in "street style" photo galleries. Street style journalism captures the dynamics between notions of organic, subcultural expressivity along with the politics and economics of Black visibility, especially within the world of fashion photography. Street style photography invokes the tension between questions of authenticity and commodification inherent in any discussion of Afropunk. Street style photography typically captures images of fashionable people as they go about their day. A visual version of "man-on-the-street" journalism, these images are meant to capture the everyday. Stylishly dressed "ordinary" people are asked to pose for a head-to-toe photograph to show their outfit. The pictures are typically framed to include the subjects' environment—a sidewalk, a café, a park, brick walls, pavement, and other urban landscapes. In some sense, the framing of the environment surrounding the image is as central to the meaning of the photo as the subjects' clothing. These images imbue an organic sense of style that the photographer may have happened upon, thereby transcending fashion photography as either art or advertisement. However, this sense is often just an illusion. Street style photos on the internet are now highly staged affairs, and in some cases, street-style models congregate in prized locations waiting to be discovered. Therefore, the production of these images can be highly circumscribed by their ubiquitous genre conventions.

I also conducted searches on Instagram and Pinterest, two highly visual social media platforms, for the hashtag #Afropunk. Instagram and Pinterest are the second and third most popular social network platforms used on both smartphones and desktop computers (Casey 2016). Instagram is a social media platform that allows users to post photos they have taken, which can then be changed with special filters. Instagram emphasizes the user's creative alteration of photography, and allows anyone with a camera phone to produce images that were once the domain of professionals. These images are collected on the user's Instagram page, which, if viewed together, offers a curated glimpse into the user's interests. Viewers can also comment on and "like" images to indicate their shared interest in it. Pinterest is a social media platform that allows users to "pin" images they find online onto a digital vision board. Users develop pages relating to various personal themes, and they can search for and share content with other users by pinning content from other boards. Like other social media platforms, content is searchable by hashtag, and viewers show their interest in an image by pinning it to their pages. Both Instagram and Pinterest emphasize the image over text. They have both been adopted by ordinary people who wish to share aspects of their lives with others, but they are also used as monetizing tools for corporations and celebrities for promotional purposes.

To catalog the images I found, I curated a personal page on Pinterest, entitled "the Mothership." Viewers of my page read my description: "Afrofuturism meets Afropunk, and they have a love-child who lives in space." On this page, I have collected images related to my intersecting interests in Black women, Afrofuturism, and Afropunk. The title "the Mothership" is derived from the funk music trope made most popular by Parliament Funkadelic's album *The Mothership Connection*. However, I have worked to reorient this Afrofuturistic trope around images of Black womanhood, as a means of thinking through Black women's artistic output as a kind of "mothership connection" that draws on themes of maternity as creativity (David 2016). My personal Pinterest page allows me to engage in the curatorial process as an ordinary user and researcher, which also informs how I think about the *processes* of building visual content that reflects an Afropunk aesthetic. Altogether, these media collections and fashion journalism, as well as my own practice of collecting and curating a Pinterest page, have generated the themes I have identified. All of the images discussed in this chapter can be found on my personal Pinterest page located at https://www.pinterest.com/marlodavid/the -mothership/.

The importance of *Hairstyle* as a theme in Black women's Afropunk citizenship can be first seen in an August 2014 *Vogue* photo essay (Carlos 2014). The publication produced a slideshow of twenty-eight photographs of Afropunk attendees taken by up-and-coming multimedia artist Awol Erizku. The convergence of Afropunk Fest, art-world darling Erizku, and the venerable fashion magazine *Vogue* operates as a critical starting point of examination in part because it marks my first contact with coverage of Afropunk in mainstream online fashion-oriented publications. Prior to 2014, online coverage of Afropunk primarily appeared in music-centered magazines, such as *Billboard* and *Rolling Stone*, and typical photo coverage featured the musical acts performing at the festival more than images of festival style. This convergence—Afropunk, visual artist, and fashion photography—also materially enacts the ways that media outlets comb diasporic Black culture (both photographer and photographic subjects) looking for the "next big thing." Yet, for participants in the portraits as well as the artist himself, the experience may have marked an opportunity for mass visibility that transcends the community directly attending the festival each summer as an act of cultural citizenship. Erizku, who was born in Ethiopia and raised in the Bronx, describes an artistic desire to "illuminate the fractal symmetry of black hair and the sentiment attached" (Carlos 2014). In that vein, each individual was photographed against a bright, warm yellow background, an orange background, or a blue background that highlighted Erizku's eye for black hair. In many cases, the subject is facing away from the camera so that the back of the head is visible, and thereby emphasizing the importance of *Hairstyle*. In some cases, however, the subject is photographed face-forward or in profile so that *Hairstyle* and *Body Modification* are visible. The portrait series operates at two registers: the spectacular, especially in light of the growing interest in natural hair and recent commentaries about the impulse for white people to try to touch Black women's hair. But the photos also act as a marking, an acknowledgment, a loving homage. While every portrait captures the startling, fierce beauty of Blackness, several stand out for closer reading.

First, a model named Reign appears with the sides of her head shaved bald and accented by a topknot of white wavy hair accented with black strands that extend past her shoulders. Reign is adorned with a septum piercing (an earring placed between her nostrils) and chains that attach to her earlobes. She has bright red designs painted on her forehead that look like the detailed henna motifs used in some Indian and Arab communities. She is copiously adorned with beads, sequins, and crystals, which reflect goddess-based spiritual traditions that emphasize crystals as transmitters of living frequencies and a connection with the earth. Reign's heavily embellished hair and body fill up Erizku's frame, and her direct stare into the lens appears to challenge the viewer to notice every detail of her style. In subsequent years, Reign has appeared in several fashion photo galleries documenting the Afropunk festival, and her image also appears on many Black women's Afropunk Pinterest boards. In some ways, her magical look has become synonymous with Afropunk.

In another image by Erizku, jewelry designer Fanta poses in profile to show the detail of the concentric circles made by her hair. Her thick, dark brown locs are coiled around her head in Bantu knots, which are then held together with a bit of copper wire. Fanta describes her self-styling as "the 'cosmic crown.' It's Afrofuturism on the head" (Carlos 2014). In this case, Fanta identifies her Afrofuturistic inspiration for her crowning glory. Her invocation of a cosmic motivation for her hair is spiritual, even as the style itself reflects a kind of technical geometry to secure it in place. Her coils also subtly signify the two rounded buns worn by Princess Leia in the *Star Wars* film franchise. Fanta's locs both seem familiar and distant at the same time.

Locs return as a centerpiece hairstyle in an image of an unnamed woman who appears against a bright blue background styled minimally in comparison to others. Her pink- and purple-tinted locs hang just to her shoulders, and her eyes are covered with a pair of steampunk-inspired goggles. Steampunk is a subgenre of urban fiction that often joins futuristic narratives with a fascination with Victorian-era fashion and invention. The round, brass-rimmed goggles are common in steampunk cosplay communities, and Black steampunk fans have developed the alternative term "steam funk" as a means of marking Black difference. The unnamed photo subject has multicolored tattoos on both of her upper arms, and wears three piercings in her nose. She also wears white paint dotted along her eyebrow ridge and a small white stripe between her bottom lip and chin. These painted marks are meant to resemble the face painting traditions of several African ethnic groups, and they have become common forms of *Body*

Modification for Afropunk women. This steampunk subject against the blue background appears relatively understated in contrast to the layered adornment worn by Reign. However, each image collected by Erizku establishes the common aesthetic markers seen in other Afropunk images online. As one of the first fashion-forward photo galleries about the festival appearing in a mainstream publication, it also marks a shift in the way Afropunk has been marketed among its many admirers.

In a more recent photo essay by photographer Tyler Joe, appearing in *Elle*, the photographer's emphasis on *Hairstyle* is communicated in the cropping of the street style image. For example, images that highlight the subject's hair are cropped at the shoulders or above. This editorial decision can be read in contrast to images in which the full body is shown or, in some cases, the subject's hair is actually cut off in the image in order to focus on the subject's body or clothing. None of the images in this gallery have titles, captions, or names of the subjects, lending to a singular focus on the aesthetic rather than con-textualizing the individuals who have donned these looks. *Elle* posted sixty-four photographs taken by Joe at Afropunk Brooklyn 2017, and all are offered in the street style conventions, staged outside with the festival as the backdrop.

Of the dozens of images that centralize *Hairstyle*, there are several that reflect the imagery and iconography included in the Erizku gallery from *Vogue*. For example, in one image, a Black woman subject is photographed in profile so that the design of her cropped purple hair is highlighted. On the side of her head, several shaved lines cascade down toward the nape of her neck while swirled shaved designs ascend toward the crown. She wears large hoop earrings, and several small piercings in her earlobe and nose. She is photographed with her mouth open in a smile, giving a sense of joyous revelry. The whimsical purple swirled coif and her smile encode a sense of playfulness and affirmation against the backdrop of trees in the festival park.

Brightly colored hair is a consistent theme in the *Elle* style gallery. In another image, a woman stands looking off at a distance. She wears large royal blue braided hair extensions, and each braid is thick and falls just below her breasts. Gold flowers are attached throughout the braids, and a crown of gold flowers is worn on top. Floral crowns are common Afropunk style theme for hair embellishments in many of the images I have collected. Interestingly, this image is incongruous with other photos captured by Joe because amidst the quirky, bright blue hair and gold flowers, the subject's face seems forlorn and distant. Unlike many of the other images capturing pleasurable expressions, this subject strikes a dour pose. I read this visage as a subversion of the white viewer's gaze in expectation of revelry, dancing, and laughter at the Afropunk festival. As a Black woman photographed for a mainstream publication, she presents a counter-narrative of unadulterated Black abandon, and instead demonstrates the complexity of Black visual affirmation codes. The ability to self-define contributes to the photo's visual significance.

Colored hair extensions also play with notions of authenticity and artificiality of Black women's hair, often signifying the current global focus on Black women's "natural" hair. The natural hair movement privileges curly and kinky textured hair that is unprocessed by chemical straighteners, and hair care routines emphasize the use of organic products. While this natural hair movement has been seen as an affirmational step toward appreciating Black beauty in the face of dominant white beauty standards, many Black women have pushed back against the regime of authenticity encoded by the natural hair movement. As a result, Black women may choose to wear their hair in multiple styles throughout the year, sometimes in its natural state, sometimes straightened, and at other times wearing wigs, weaves, or hair extensions. Often in everyday situations, when Black women and girls change their styles, they are questioned about their versatile hair or accused of being inauthentic or fake by trying to pass off wigs, weaves, and extensions as real hair. When these hair choices are made, people often question their authenticity by asking, "Is your hair real?" or focus on the hypervisibility of Black women's hair by asking, "How do you get your hair like that?"

In light of these hair politics, I read the phenomenon of brightly colored hair extensions and wigs as forms of Afropunk hair aesthetics that put the artificiality of the hair front and center and harkens to hairstyling practices associated with working-class Black women. In several of Joe's images from *Elle*, Black women are pictured with brightly colored braids and goddess locs, with their black and brown hair roots exposed. In one particularly striking image, a festival goer wearing pineapple-shaped sunglass frames wears her multicolored braids coiled up into two buns on her head. At the roots, you can see her dark brown hair woven in with the strands of turquoise, green, and hot pink synthetic hair. As brightly colored hair extensions are braided or twisted into dark colored curly or kinky hair, those roots are not hidden. Instead they bring attention to the fact that the extensions are artificial. This choice of choosing hypervisible hair and accentuating its artificiality plays with the questions of "real" Black hair, and highlights the flexibility and fun available in Black women's hairstyles. Black women's Afropunk aesthetics include hypervisibility of hairstyles, redefining the meanings of wigs, weaves, and extensions as techniques solely meant to hide or conceal the "ugliness" of natural Black hair. Rather, they are seen as embellishments, as a kind of cyborg fusion of the synthetic and organic that inspires creativity and speaks to the DIY spirit of punk looks.

Likewise, free-form or organic locs like the ones on Fanta in the Erizku *Vogue* essay appear in various #Afropunk online spaces. Free-form locs are dreadlocked Black hair that is not "trained" by twisting the roots to create uniformity in the hair. Instead the dreadlocks are allowed to grow in any size and direction. These locs may be worn for spiritual reasons, such as within Rastafarian communities, or as a personal subversion of the recent trend to wear tightly groomed dreads that require more maintenance in order for them to be deemed acceptable. In one image in the *Elle* photo gallery, two Black women with free-form locs stand shoulder to shoulder in an embrace. One woman's thick matted hair is coiled high up on her head, while the other's falls loosely down her shoulders. In an image appearing in the *Allure* photo spread, a woman named Amanda appears with her dreadlocks twisted together into two "sculptural horns" that rise up above her head (Elizabeth and Menghistab 2017). In both of these instances, free-form locs challenge the norms of *respectable* Black hair.

Conclusion

This chapter explores the visual sites of #BlackGirlMagic as expressed in the contemporary phenomenon of the global Afropunk movement, which includes music festivals throughout the year and an online presence in several platforms. I began by identifying the common threads between the identification of #BlackGirlMagic and other affirmation codes circulating in millennial digital spaces as counter-hegemonic sites for identifying Black women's agency, creativity, and self-definition. I contend that the affirmation codes that appear as hashtags across the internet can be potentially visualized and mate-rialized through the phenomenon of Afropunk. I then discuss how Afropunk formed as a cultural movement, first through the produc-tion of a documentary that placed Black individuals at the center of punk history and further through the establishment of IRL and online activities to create community from these affinities. The growth of Afropunk has been both celebrated and critiqued, and I posit that even with its commercialization, Afropunk marks a kind of affec-tive resistance work in light of global anti-Black racism and violence. "Afropunk has created something that is 100% theirs—bringing people of color together in a country that has shown time and time again that they will be hunted down. To adorn, strut, and celebrate black and brown bodies at a time when they are under attack is a subversive act. It's punk as fuck" (Cepeda 2017).

Further, I contend that much more work needs to be done to delineate how Black women enter Afropunk spaces and how they use it collectively in their political and aesthetic resistance practices. To produce this gendered analysis of Afropunk aesthetics, I collected digital images of Black women and femme people via the social media site Pinterest. I then used these images to produce close readings. At the end of this chapter, I identified Black women's hairstyles as a primary theme for understanding Afropunk citizenship as a site of diasporic belonging. The transmission and exchange of images of Black women's hairstyles through the use of the hashtag #Afropunk, and through social media and fashion journalism, both mark and generate spaces of belonging for millennial Black women.

Overall, my analysis seeks to contribute to an understanding of what #BlackGirlMagic looks like, by tracing the ways that the hashtag itself operates as an affirmation code that can be tracked throughout digital spaces as a way to create community with other Black women. While the exact dimensions of #BlackGirlMagic have yet to be defined—as if that is even possible—I contend that Afropunk aesthetics, particularly regarding Black women's hairstyles, produces a visual affirmation code akin to #BlackGirlMagic. Taking up Conley's important work on Black code, I assert that Afropunk and #BlackGirlMagic work in tandem

> as visual dimensions of code, [they] shake loose dominant logics to reveal new(er) relations that sometimes form on the basis of solidarity, sometimes not. Black feminist hashtags are thresholds between dehumanization that is lived and livable; they are sites of struggle over the politics of representation. They function as a way to renew stories and

interventions across time and space. They express desires to break-through social norms of violence and marginalization, and to belong. (Conley 2017, 29)

Works Cited

Carlos, Marjon. 2014. "Forces of Nature: 28 Afropunk Hair Portraits by Artist Awol Erizku." *Vogue.* August 26. https://www.vogue.com/article /afropunk-festival-hair-portraits-awol-erizku.

Casey, Shawn. 2016. "2016 Nielsen Social Media Report." Nielson Social. January 17. http://www.nielsen.com/us/en/insights/reports/2017/2016-nielsen -social-media-report.html.

Cepeda, Eddie. 2017. "If Afropunk Isn't Punk Anymore, What Is It?" *Track-Record.* September 8. https://trackrecord.net/if-afropunk-isnt-punk-any more-what-is-it-1818879972/.

Chatelain, Marcia, and Kaavya Asoka. 2015. "Women and Black Lives Matter." *Dissent* 62 (3): 54–61.

Chavers, Linda. 2016. "Here's My Problem with #BlackGirlMagic." *Elle.* January 13. http://www.elle.com/life-love/a33180/why-i-dont-love-blackgirl magic/.

Clarke, Kamari M. 2013. "Notes on Cultural Citizenship in the Black Atlantic World." *Cultural Anthropology* 28 (3): 464–74.

Conley, Tara L. 2017. "Decoding Black Feminist Hashtags as Becoming." *Black Scholar* 47 (3): 22–32.

David, Marlo D. 2016. *Mama's Gun: Black Maternal Figures and the Politics of Transgression.* Columbus: Ohio State University Press.

Donnley, Ebony. 2018. "Afropunk Doesn't Care about Black People: Beyond a T-shirt." *Medium.* August 31. https://medium.com/@ebonypdonnley_58428 /afropunk-doesnt-care-about-black-people-beyond-a-t-shirt-a5a7d63de09f/.

Elizabeth, De, and Meron Menghistab. 2017. "28 of the Best Street Style Looks We Saw at Afropunk." *Allure.* August 28. https://www.allure.com/gallery /afropunk-2017-best-dressed-street-style/.

Ellis, Trey. 1989. "The New Black Aesthetic." *Callaloo* 38: 233–43.

Fields, Rob. 2016. "The Evolution of Afropunk." *Forbes.* September 1. https:// www.forbes.com/sites/robfields/2016/09/01/the-evolution-of-afropunk/2 /#42464fbd20d5/.

Ford, Tanisha C. 2015. *Liberated Threads: Black Women, Style, and the Global Politics of Soul*. Chapel Hill: University of North Carolina Press.

Hope, Clover. 2017. "Who Gets to Own 'Black Girl Magic'?" *Jezebel*. https://jezebel.com/who-gets-to-own-black-girl-magic-1793924053.

Johnson, Jessica Marie, and Mark Anthony Neal. 2017. "Introduction: Wild Seed in the Machine." *Black Scholar* 47 (3): 1–2.

Josephs, Brian. 2015. "Is Afropunk Fest No Longer Punk?" *Vice*. August 17. https://www.vice.com/en_us/article/qbxjx7/is-the-afropunk-festival-no-longer-punk-813/.

Kameir, Rawiya. 2015. "The True Story of How Afropunk Turned a Message Board Into a Movement." *FADER*. August 21. http://www.thefader.com/2015/08/21/james-spooner-afropunk/.

Lindsey, Treva B. 2018. "Ain't Nobody Got Time for That: Anti-Black Girl Violence in the Era of #SayHerName." *Urban Education* 53 (2): 162–75.

Mbembe, Achille. 2003. "Necropolitics." *Public Culture* 15 (1): 11–40.

Smith, Christen A. 2015. "Blackness, Citizenship, and the Transnational Vertigo of Violence in the Americas." *American Anthropologist* 117 (2): 384–87.

Spooner, James, dir. 2003. *Afro-Punk*. Documentary. Image Entertainment.

Tate, Greg. 2011. "Of Afropunks and Other Anarchic Signifiers of Contrary Negritude." In *From Bourgeois to Boojie: Black Middle-Class Performances*, edited by Vershawn Ashanti Young and Bridget Harris Tsemo, 155–58. Detroit, Mich.: Wayne State University Press.

CHAPTER 7

DAUGHTER ⟳ MOTHER

An Intergenerational Conversation on
the Meaning of #BlackGirlMagic

Makeen J. Zachery and Julia S. Jordan-Zachery

According to KaaVonia Hinton-Johnson, "One of the most significant familial relationships in black women's literature is the one that
exists between mothers and daughters" (2004). As reported by Anita
Jones Thomas and Constance T. King, in their study on race-gender
socialization, "Daughters experience and process the socialization as
mothers intended, as both reported similar messages, particularly
the importance of self-determination and self-pride" (2007, 140).
Mothering is a complex phenomenon—one shaped by race, class,
gender, and other identity markers. As a mother of a young Black
woman, I am constantly wondering if I have done the right thing by
enrolling my child in a predominantly white school—a space where
she often finds herself the lone Black girl. I also wonder what it means
that we have no community that grounds her in my identity as a
Barbadian woman. Will she know my dialect or my food? Will she
understand my socialization as I try to raise her in a post-9/11 context
where her life has been one in which war has been a constant and
Black death resulting from state violence is ever present? How will
she understand and perform her identity? These are questions that I
often ponder as I mother this young Black woman.

I watch her evolve and her consciousness take shape. Her ability
to be grounded in her identity is assuring. She meanders beautifully

through various spaces and seems to be grounded in a Black feminist sensibility that centers justice and equity. The genesis of this project emerged from many conversations with my daughter, particularly conversations related to her identity. I admit that I was particularly skeptical about #BlackGirlMagic and its prevalence in digital spaces. My daughter, Makeen, has a relatively substantial presence on Twitter. She tweets primarily about Black girls and culture. Due to my limited use of Twitter, I was unaware that her tweets have been published or shared in magazines like *Complex* and the *New York Times*. It was time for me to reverse the role of the mother guiding and/or teaching the daughter and sit and listen to my child's experiences with her identity, particularly in digital spaces such as Twitter.

Below is the conversation we shared on the meaning of #Black-GirlMagic. As you read this, you will see that there is an accompanied soundtrack. As we talked, Makeen would intersperse the conversation with snippets of songs. What is fascinating to me is the nature of the songs; they tell their own stories—why she consciously or unconsciously selected certain songs and how she wove them around her tale of identity and Black-gendered consciousness is sometimes known to me and at other times it all remains a mystery.

I don't want to be like Cinderella
Sittin' in a dark cold dusty cellar
Waitin' for somebody to come and set me free

Don't want to be no no no one else
I'd rather rescue myself.
—CHEETAH GIRLS, "CINDERELLA"

Makeen somehow would stress the "no, no, no" so it sounded like "NO, NO, NO!" She hums along as I pose the first question.

When you hear the term *BlackGirlMagic* what does it mean to you?

Makeen J. Zachery: BlackGirlMagic, to me, encompasses a wide range of [*pause*] qualities, I guess, that Black women bring to everything that they do. Be it through art, writing, preforming, or through politics and, um, other things [*soft chuckle*]. How about you?

Julia S. Jordan-Zachery: I have to be honest. When I first became aware of the term BlackGirlMagic I was a little [*pause*], not suspect, but it didn't really capture my imagination. Um, because I thought it didn't really capture the work that Black women do to make themselves whole. To make themselves visible. To make themselves, um [*thought fades out*]. To create themselves in a way that's true and honest to them in an organic way. This is why I started this project, because I was really curious about what it is that BlackGirlMagic means. And so, I started doing lots of research and I realized that Black women have been talking about magic for quite some time. And, um, it's their way of saying that in spite of all of the structures imposed on us, here we are. So, it's not necessarily a mythical figure, which is how I originally thought of it, right. That there is mysticism involved. But it's a kinda way of, of making themselves real. And so that's how I think about it at this point, but I have to admit that I had to evolve into seeing it that way.

As we prepare to transition to the next question she continues to sing "Cinderella," stressing that she can save herself. I sit quietly listening to her sing.

Has the term been commercialized in your view? And if so, how? And is it a problem if it's commercialized?

MZ: I think that BlackGirlMagic as [*thought fades*]—looking at it as a movement, as I do, I do think that it has become commercialized in some way. Because, you know, you see it on T-shirts you can purchase. It's being used by companies that aren't even Black-owned anymore; I dunno, it's just being used by people to get our support and our money. But I don't think that the roots of this movement have been commercialized. I do think it's expanded in a way that it may not have meant to originally. However, I believe the roots of supporting sisterhood and excellence and the achievements of Black girls are still present. And when used by Black women it stays true to those original goals.

As I think about how to answer this question, she picks back up her soundtrack, humming lyrics this time.

JZ: Has it been commercialized?

MZ: Tell us what you think? [*both chuckle*]

JZ: To some extent [*with laughter*] I think it has been commercialized. But that's kind of the work that Black women do, right. Oftentimes the work that Black women do, to bring themselves into being, gets taken from them, um, taken to be used by other people's purposes. So yes, they put the image of BlackGirlMagic and all these different images of Black girls and women on T-shirts and earrings and bags, etcetera. But, the key thing for me, which I think BlackGirlMagic is about, which people don't always think about, is oppressive structures, right. And so, when that terminology becomes commercialized and we fail to look at the oppressive structures that Black women have to exist in that's where the problem is for me. Less so in the commercialization but what commercialization doesn't allow us to see. So BlackGirlMagic on a T-shirt doesn't allow us to see [*I laugh as she makes a face at me*] how Black women are dying; for example, in childbirth. And those are the challenging kind[s] of topics that I think get disappeared in a catch term.

MZ: But . . . can I respond?

JZ: Yes, we can go back and forth.
[*This time there is no accompanying soundtrack or laughter.*]

MZ: I don't think that BlackGirlMagic is ignoring issues like that. Even if it hadn't been commercialized, I think this would still be an issue. BlackGirlMagic doesn't focus on the fact that Black women are dying in child labor; it doesn't really focus on the problems that society places on us for being Black women and girls. But it focuses on the great things we do in spite of those challenges. So, I don't see it as an issue of commercialization or that we are not seeing the whole childbirth example, or that we are not seeing the issues facing Black women in certain countries. What BlackGirlMagic is saying is that despite all of these challenges, these stigmas, and these stereotypes that are placed against Black women to limit us, we still do and achieve great things, which is almost magical [*pause*]. Hence the magic in BlackGirlMagic.

JZ: So, how is it then that Black women can have the opportunity to talk about these types of issues that are killing us? Because, yes, we might be able to have some form of success given everything that we face, but that success comes at a cost. So where in BlackGirlMagic are we allowed to talk about the cost carried by Black women and girls when we are "magical"?

Soundtrack changes. She now sings.

See she's telepathic
Call it black girl magic
—JAMILIA WOODS, "BLK GIRL SOLDIER"

MZ: Well, I don't think that BlackGirlMagic has to include all of that because BlackGirlMagic is not the only thing that Black women have. And it's not the only platform we have to speak about things. I think the one thing that is beautiful about Black women, which BlackGirl-Magic highlights, is that we are able to do so many different things, and to have so many discussions and to lead so many causes. So, just because BlackGirlMagic itself doesn't address many of the problems that face us doesn't mean we aren't talking about them and that we are not able to talk about them. And I think that as Black women we are capable of simultaneously supporting and applauding our successes, our beauty, and our talents while also talking about the structures within which we live that are hurting us and causing us harm.

JZ: So, what is a comparable hashtag to #BlackGirlMagic that allows us to explore the kind of pain? Or do you think that there isn't, um, a comparable hashtag because confronting the pain, the cost associated with being a Black girl and a Black woman, is just too high for us to put out in Twitter, [in the] Twitterverse, or whatever you want to call it?

MZ: Well I don't think that it has to be a hashtag necessarily. But if we are speaking of social media activism, if that's what you want to call it, there are hashtags that do exist that allow Black women to talk about their problems, and there are also pages that exist, whether they have set names or not, that are out there. So, I think a hashtag in which these discussions are happening, like #SayHerName talks about police brutality. I think women are increasingly becoming more included in the Black Lives Matter movement discussions and I'm sure that there are some pages or hashtags that I don't even know about that exist. I think the beautiful thing about platforms like Twitter is that it is so easy to have discussions whether or not you want to name it with a hashtag. There are people out there that do want to talk and do talk about it. Because it's not featured in BlackGirlMagic specifically doesn't mean that it's not happening and that the same people participating in BlackGirlMagic discussions may be having these other discussions elsewhere.

She picks back up the song "Blk Girl Soldier."

Does the term *girl* imply a limit as to who can use it? If not, why?

MZ: NO! Because, I think Black women refer to each other as *girl* all the time [*smiling as she makes this assertion*]. Whether it is literally a child or a friend who is their own age. I don't think *girl* implies an age. I think it's a term of endearment for Black women. And maybe always has been but I'm not sure the history of that.

JZ: Why do you think the term *girl* is used? Is it kind of a subversive term? How do you—what work does that allow us to do? Because she could have picked a different terminology to use as opposed to "Black Girls are Magic." Why do you think that term resonates so much?

MZ: My first response is I have no idea [*we stop and giggle*]. I guess in thinking about it, the term *girl* implies some form of youthfulness that Black women have, I guess adopted over time. Because we are expected to and we do most of the work in various settings that require some kind of energy, some sort of—I guess you can say youthfulness that the term *girl* encompasses. However [*dramatic pause*], I don't know [*smiles*].

We have this intense moment of teasing each other and laughing. What was so funny? Makeen is mimicking me as she reposes the question.

JZ: I think *girl* stretches beyond boundaries of what society has imposed on us and told us what behaviors are acceptable, etc. And so, I think it's a way of Black women [*laughter*] bending, resisting, contorting, um, time, age, sensibility. I think they are claiming a past, thinking about a present, and creating a future where certain boundaries that are imposed on us don't exist.

Michelle Obama (2015), in a speech at the Black Girls Rock! Awards, said that young Black girls often hear "voices that tell you that you're not good enough, that you have to look a certain way, act a certain way; that if you speak up, you're too loud; if you step up to lead, you're being bossy." How do you respond to this claim?

MZ: I don't think that Michelle Obama spoke incorrectly about what Black girls hear; whether it is someone literally telling them that they are too loud or that they are taking up too much space. Or whether it is just society shaping us into thinking that we need to behave a certain way. So, I think that it's true and it's sad that Black girls and women throughout their lifetime are often told to limit themselves, to make themselves smaller literally and figuratively regardless of the spaces they are taking up. And it shouldn't be that way, but it definitely is.

JZ: I have had multiple experiences of people attempting to tell me to be quiet when I dare speak up against structures and policies that harm Black women. I've received these messages from white folks; I've received them from Black folks, regardless of gender. I often hear "Julia is a troublemaker." The same people who would say I'm a troublemaker often remain silent about the questions I'm asking, about how minoritized individuals are treated. They remain silent to my questioning of structural violence and of anti-Blackness, of racial violence. So yes, I've experienced how individuals try [*thought fades*], because it's in their interests to limit my speech, to limit my claims for the full recognition of not just my humanity but the humanity of all Black women and girls.

Do you think you are "magical" when you choose to speak up in spite of being told to be quiet, etc.?

MZ: I don't think that I myself am magical. But I do think that collectively, when Black women speak up against certain things, whether it be systemic issues or just small issues within their homes, that it is a magical thing in a way. By magical I mean that it is admirable; it's amazing how despite all of the barriers and limitations placed on us we are still able to speak up for whatever we believe in. And, so I don't [*thought shifts*] — when I myself speak up I don't think of myself as magical necessarily. However, I do think that collectively as Black women we do magical things when we use our voices. Because we are so often told not to. We are magical because we are pushing against the limitations and barriers that are placed on us in order to fight for what we believe in.

JZ: As a young Black woman, what do you believe in?

MZ: Okay, what? [*laughs*]. I believe that Black women and girls are capable of whatever they put their minds to. And so, I use hashtags like #BlackGirlMagic on my Twitter account to enforce that and to really prove that. I think that's the core of what BlackGirlMagic is. It's not that any specific actions are magical. It's just that Black women existing in the conditions that we do with the restrictions that society so often places on us, you know, our existence alone is sort of revolutionary and is magical in and of itself. So, I guess what I would fight for in terms of—what I would speak up for is definitely against the violent forms of oppression that we face, whether it be through systems like police brutality, or the healthcare system failing us. Of course, there are an array of violent systems that we exist in. But I think that at the core of it all, I definitely try to focus on the positive things that Black women create for ourselves.

"I believe in miracles"
No matter where . . .
We come from . . .
We can be ourselves . . .
And still be . . . one!
—CHEETAH GIRLS, "AMIGAS CHEETAHS"

What are the limits to BlackGirlMagic?

MZ: There are none. That's what makes it magical. There are no limits 'cause I think that it exists to contrast the society that we live in, which is filled with various limits, boundaries, and restrictions. BlackGirlMagic serves as an outlet for the emotions that you might not always be able to fairly display.

Why do you think the term BlackGirlMagic seems to resonate with Black girls AND women?

MZ: I think that as Black women and girls we very rarely receive the recognition that we deserve, or feel that we deserve, from other people. So, though this serves as something that was created for and by us to applaud us for our achievements and accomplishments and the great aspects of everything that we do, it sort of serves as a public recognition or applause for Black women. And though it was created, and at its core, exclusively for Black women, other people are able to contribute and applaud us as well. And I think [*stops to whistle*] that simply put everybody at some point wants their achievements to be acknowledged. Which BlackGirlMagic does for Black women.

Makeen decides to change the conversation. At some point the dynamic of the conversation shifts. She asks: **Do you think you are magical when you speak when others are telling you to be quiet?**

JZ: Am I magical? [*laughter*]. No. Am I honest? Yes. I choose to speak because I choose to live. I choose to resist the kind of "murder" society tries to inflict on us by using my voice. So, it's not magical, it's not brave, it's nothing spectacular to me. The only thing it is is a will to live. And I choose to speak because of my ancestors. I choose to speak for the generation that will come after me. But I choose to speak primarily for you. BECAUSE of you!

MZ: Love you, mom.
   [*We smile at each other before continuing.*]

MZ: **As a Black woman what do you believe in?**

JZ: I believe in freedom. I believe in justice. I believe in humanity. I always try to have my actions mirror my beliefs, my words mirror my beliefs. So, in everything I do, I try to work from a principal of justice and freedom, for the humanity of Black women and girls.

MZ: Why do you think that term *BlackGirlMagic* seems to resonate with Black girls and women?

JZ: Because we need something. We need something in this era that has basically disappeared us. We have been voting, we've been organizing, and we've been fighting [*long pause*]. And I think BlackGirl-Magic resonates because it says to Black women and girls, "I see you, I see you and I honor you for who and what you are." Now, do I think that BlackGirlMagic is also a little superficial? Yes [*quiet as we gaze at each other*]. But I also recognize its value. And it's sad that in 2017 Black women and girls still have to fight to be seen.

There is another shift, but this time it's not accompanied by a song.

How, if at all, is this [BlackGirlMagic] a political statement?

MZ: I think BlackGirlMagic is political because it stands up against all that Black women and girls are told not to be. Kinda as I've been saying, society wants Black women and girls to behave in a certain way to serve a certain purpose and not to step outside of those boundaries. And BlackGirlMagic not only allows Black women and girls to escape those boundaries [*pause*] and not only creates a space in which Black women are allowed to exist without these restrictions, but in creating said space, it speaks up and challenges the societal norms that have been in existence for so long.

JZ: I think BlackGirlMagic is probably more cultural than political. It becomes political when it is translated into specific types of actions of resistance. And I'm not suggesting that there isn't any value in cultural resistance. So, for example, there is value in the song "I'm black and I'm proud. Say it loud." So, I think of BlackGirlMagic like that. However, I am kind of concerned in terms of it being political because I'm not sure, beyond its cultural relevance, what it's allowing us to build. What is it allowing us to do to challenge structures?

[*I search really hard for my words while answering this question.*]

MZ: Can I respond? Are you ready? In response to the question about what BlackGirlMagic allows us to build, I don't think that everything Black people create for ourselves has to create political change. I think that [*pause*] Black culture has always existed hand in hand with Black political resistance and movements. Hashtags or trends like #BlackGirlMagic exist to feed the emotional and physical exhaustion that can come from existing as a Black woman in this society. So, though BlackGirlMagic may not necessarily create political change directly, I think it does function politically in that it serves the people who are creating the change. Which Black women always have been.

Conclusion

JZ: What is fascinating, is that she [Makeen] too searches for her words as she responds. She ends by humming a tune that I can't identify. I choose to let her be with her song as I let her be with her vision of self and community.

MZ: Shout out to Mom for always representing BlackGirlMagic for me. I think that without relationships like mother-daughter,

grandmother-daughter, aunt-niece, you know, those familial relationships, without those relationships we won't have a base for
#BlackGirlMagic.

Works Cited

Hinton-Johnson, KaaVonia. 2004. "African American Mothers & Daughters:
 Socialization, Distance, & Conflict." *Alan Review* 31 (3). https://scholar.lib
 .vt.edu/ejournals/ALAN/v31n3/hintonjohnson.html.

Jones Thomas, Anita, and Constance T. King. 2007. "Gendered Racial Socialization of African American Mothers and Daughters." *Family Journal* 15
 (2): 137–42.

Obama, Michelle. 2015. Remarks by the First Lady at BET's "Black Girls
 Rock!" event. https://obamawhitehouse.archives.gov/the-press-office/2015
 /03/28/remarks-first-lady-bets-black-girls-rock-event/.

AFTERWORD

BlackGirlMagic Is Real

Tammy Owens

I'm poor, black, and I may even be ugly, but dear God, I'm here. I'm here.
—MISS CELIE, *THE COLOR PURPLE*

It is significant that this anthology opens with a nod to both CaShawn Thompson for her theory of #BlackGirlMagic as well as Alice Walker's early recognition of Black women's magic in 1983. Among many reasons besides citation, it is important to mention Walker because her book, which was turned into a motion picture, became one of the most important representations of Black women and girls claiming power to name themselves and survive at the intersections of racism, sexism, and poverty in the United States. Like the concept #Black-GirlMagic, it caused an uproar and incited heated debates about the authenticity of Black women's narratives of survival against the odds.

Oftentimes when scholars examine Walker's character Miss Celie, in the novel *The Color Purple* or the motion picture version, they speak of "Miss Celie's Blues." They speak of "Miss Celie's Blues" to reference the endearing title of the song that the stunning, headstrong, and wandering character Shug Avery sings, or in the long, suffering years throughout her life that Miss Celie experienced myriad forms of abuse from men, especially her husband, Mr. ___. Most of the scholarly focus has been on the latter reference. While it is true that Miss

Celie certainly had a life story that was rife with the blues, it is also true that Miss Celie was magical. Interestingly, Celie discovers her magic in many of the same ways that the authors of this anthology illuminate in their work—in collaboration with other Black girls and women. That is, Celie is able to see, name, and practice her magic in the collective world that she and Shug Avery create to escape and share Mr. ___. Together, Shug Avery and Miss Celie find power to define themselves. As they conjure together, the women birth self-definitions that are free from the world of men and oppressors like Mr. ___. In this new world of self-discovery, Mr. ___ is not relevant.

Like Miss Celie and Shug Avery, through historical trajectories of BlackGirlMagic, empirical research, and meditations, the essays in this anthology work together to provide readers of various backgrounds with the tools needed to see, theorize, and practice Black-GirlMagic. As the collection of essays illuminate, the ingenuity and creativity of Black girls and women have been invaluable to American culture. Yet, the terms *genius* or *innovator* or others, such as *intellectual* and *theorist*, are rarely attributed to Black women and girls. Black girls and women have rightfully chosen to move beyond dominant categories to name, define, and theorize themselves and their work. In their resistance movements outside of these categories, they have found ways to speak and identify their creativity and experiences as constituting BlackGirlMagic. Readers of this collection should be encouraged to use the essays as tangible proof of how one can put magic into words and show that BlackGirlMagic is not a transient concept in the world of hashtags. Rather, BlackGirlMagic is real, and Black girls and women have the interminable right to always name, define, and theorize its dimensions.

Once Miss Celie sees her magic, she finds the words to stand up to her abusers, and most importantly, she learns to put her magic into practice by stepping out of bondage and into the world with Shug Avery. Her practice of daily survival and ability to exist or be *here*, despite Mr. ___'s claim that she, in fact, cannot exist as Black, poor, and a woman, resonates with the Black girls and women practicing magic throughout this anthology. Contributors' chapters explain how Black girls' daily existence and artistic rituals allow them to practice their magic. Furthermore, they reveal the adaptability of Black girls and women's performances of magic by demonstrating the ways in which BlackGirlMagic can be used to survive within institutions that are not intended to sustain the lives of Black women and girls. Yet, Black girls and women survive. Despite all of the odds, they are here.

Works Cited

Spielberg, Steven, dir. 1985. *The Color Purple*. Screenplay by Menno Meyjes. Warner Bros., Amblin Entertainment.
Walker, Alice. 1982. *The Color Purple*. Orlando, Fla.: Harcourt.

CONTRIBUTORS

Abena Amory-Powell is a graduate of SUNY Downstate School of Public Health where she received her MPH in community health sciences. She also earned her BA in social deviance from John Jay College of Criminal Justice. She has been actively involved in advocacy, community engagement, and community service. Becoming a part of the team at a grassroots nonprofit organization helped her realize her passion for advocacy and social justice. She has been working in communities in central Brooklyn, New York, bringing awareness to the traumatic effects that violence has on communities and helping neighborhoods heal and transform.

Marlo D. David is the director of the African American Studies Research Center and an associate professor of English and women's, gender, and sexuality studies at Purdue University. Her research focuses on contemporary African American literature and culture and their intersections with political and social movements, and Black feminist gender and sexuality studies. She is the author of *Mama's Gun: Black Maternal Figures and the Politics of Transgression*, which examines how writers use representations of transgressive Black motherhood to challenge neoliberalism. Her scholarly essays have appeared in *Tulsa Studies of Women's Literature, Black Camera: An International Film Journal, African American Review*, and *Home Girls Make Some Noise: A Hip Hop Feminist Anthology*. She is currently working on a book about the writer, actor, and filmmaker Bill Gunn.

LeConté J. Dill was born and raised in South Central Los Angeles and is currently creating a homeplace in Bed-Stuy Brooklyn. She is a scholar, educator, and a poet in and out of classroom and community spaces. She holds degrees from Spelman College, UCLA, and UC Berkeley, was a health policy postdoctoral fellow at Morehouse School of Medicine, and a 2016 Callaloo Creative Writing Workshop Fellow. Currently, she is the director of public health practice and a clinical associate professor of social and behavioral sciences at the New York University College of Global Public Health. Additionally, since 2015, she has been a research associate at the African Centre for Migration & Society at Wits University in Johannesburg, South Africa. Committed to practicing what she names as #CrunkPublicHealth, her community-accountable scholarship is focused on addressing health inequities and fostering protective factors among urban youth of color. Guided by Black feminist epistemologies, her recent work documents urban Black girls' strategies of resilience, safety, and wellness.

Porshé R. Garner received her PhD in educational policy studies with a graduate minor in gender and women's studies from the University of Illinois Urbana-Champaign. Her work interrogates Black girlhood spirituality as it is practiced in the collective SOLHOT (Saving Our Lives Hear Our Truths) and beyond. More specifically, she is interested in how otherworld making through the metaphysical and futurity is made possible through the lived experiences and relationships created and maintained through Black girlhood. She is currently the executive director of the Art Film Foundation in Champaign, Illinois.

Duchess Harris is a professor of American studies at Macalester College. She was a Mellon Mays fellow at the University of Pennsylvania. She graduated with a degree in American history. She earned a PhD in American studies from the University of Minnesota and a JD from William Mitchell College of Law. She became the first chair of Macalester's American studies department in 2003. She is a scholar of contemporary African American history and political theory. Her academic books include *Racially Writing the Republic: Racists, Race Rebels, and Transformations of American Identity* (2009) and *Black Feminist Politics from Kennedy to Trump* (2018). She is also the proud curator of the *Duchess Harris Collection*, which has more than sixty books written for third through twelfth graders.

Rashida L. Harrison is an assistant professor of social relations and policy at James Madison College, Michigan State University. Her research focuses on transnational Black and multiracial feminist social movements. More specifically, she is interested in how women build coalitions across social identities, political realities, and national borders. She uses the Black British feminist movement as a case study to examines the impact of Western empire on Black women's nationality and immigration rights, reproductive justice, and agency within public organizations. Her newest research focuses on radical Black feminist self-care. She is a native New Yorker and a proud new mama.

Janell Hobson is a professor of women's, gender, and sexuality studies at the University at Albany. She is the author of two books: *Venus in the Dark: Blackness and Beauty in Popular Culture* and *Body as Evidence: Mediating Race, Globalizing Gender*. She is working on two projects under contract: a third book, *When God Lost Her Tongue: Historical Consciousness and the Black Feminist Imagination*, and an edited collection, *The Routledge Companion to Black Women's Cultural Histories*.

Charlotte E. Jacobs' research interests focus on issues of identity development and gender in education concerning adolescent girls of color, teacher education and diversity, and youth participatory action research. She is the codirector of the Independent School Teaching Residency program at the University of Pennsylvania Graduate School of Education. In the pre-K–12 world, she is the executive director of the Girls Justice League, a nonprofit organization supporting the social, educational, and economic rights of girls in Philadelphia. She is also a consultant with Teaching Girls Well Consulting and recently co-authored the book *Teaching Girls Well: How Teachers and Parents Can Reach Their Brains and Hearts*.

Julia S. Jordan-Zachery is a professor and chair of the Africana studies department at the University of North Carolina, Charlotte. Her interdisciplinary research focuses on African American women and public policy. She is also the author of the award-winning book *Black Women, Cultural Images and Social Policy* and *Shadow Bodies: Black Women, Ideology, Representation, and Politics*. She was awarded the Accinno Teaching Award from Providence College in 2015–16. She currently serves as the president of the Association for Ethnic Studies.

Tammy Owens is an assistant professor of ethnic studies and childhood studies at Hampshire College. She earned a PhD in American studies from the University of Minnesota, and an MA in women's studies from the University of Alabama. Her forthcoming monograph,

Young Revolutionaries: Black Girls and the Fight for Girlhood from Slavery to #Sayhername, focuses on the ways Black girls and women use fiction and personal narratives as creative sites to theorize their own transitions from girlhood to womanhood. She has written essays that are published in the *Journal of the History of Childhood and Youth* and *Departures in Critical Qualitative Research*.

Bianca Rivera is a current doctoral candidate in epidemiology at SUNY Downstate School of Public Health. Her research interests include psychosocial epidemiology, and for her dissertation, she is exploring mental health outcomes in family caregivers to help guide intervention strategies and self-care support. Rivera has an affinity for academia and giving back and has experience in teaching epidemiology, biostatistics, and research methods at various levels. She has both DrPH(c) and MPH degrees. She is currently an adjunct Lecturer at her alma mater, CUNY-Hunter College, where she teaches principles of epidemiology.

Jessica L. Robinson is a doctoral student at the Institute for Communications Research at the University of Illinois at Urbana-Champaign. Her work centers on the work of SOLHOT (Saving Our Lives, Hear Our Truths), a collective that celebrates Black girlhood in all of its complexities.

Shavaun S. Sutton is a critical public health scholar who holds a master of public health degree in community health sciences from SUNY Downstate School of Public Health. She has worked in public, non-profit, academic, and hospital sectors to support sustainable health improvement. Additionally, she was a 2015–16 Beyond the Bars Fellow with the Center for Justice at Columbia University. As a qualitative researcher, she works toward amplifying voices muted by oppression and marginalization. She strives to promote health equity via the analysis of nuanced narratives and lived experience.

Makeen J. Zachery is a first-year college student with a passion for social justice. She has worked with numerous organizations to advocate for Black women. Her platform, Black Girl Culture, seeks to represent the diversity and complexities of Black womanhood. Black Girl Culture has gained more than one hundred thousand Twitter followers and its content has been republished in various magazines. Through Black Girl Culture, she hopes to continue collaborating with, uplifting, and advocating for Black women's freedom and liberation.

INDEX